THE FRONT NINE

SHERRY BRADSHAW

THE FRONT NINE

Copyright ©2014 by Sherry Bradshaw

ISBN:
TRADE PAPERBACK: 978-1-939779-06-9
HARDBACK: 978-1-939779-07-6

Published by

LIFEBRIDGE

BOOKS
P.O. Box 49428
Charlotte, NC 28277

Printed in the United States of America.

DEDICATION

This book is dedicated to my family and friends.
Starting with my wonderful parents, Tom and Pat,
and my sister, Marcia. For it was the three of them
who shared a "faith in God," "small town living," and a
support system that allowed me to grow and live the
God-ordained plans for my life. Without them the
lessons and experiences would have no meaning!

To my husband Bill, and our three children—Brewer,
Thomas and Collins—who continue to love, support, and
teach me much about unconditional love, grace, mercy and
forgiveness! They know all my "warts" and love me anyway!

To my Uncle Sam and Aunt Joellen. For all of my life
they have treated me like the daughter they never had.

To my friends and "prayer warriors" who have
loved me in the best of times and the worst of times.
Friends who have often fulfilled the Scripture of "being
closer than a brother!" Bebe, Elizabeth, Steve, Aimee, Dina,
Kay, Julie, Sheryl, Shannon, Jane, Celia, Hope, Paige, Joan,
Jeremy, Lucas, Karen, Carole, Caroline, Cathy, Leslie,
Lisa, Donna, Tonja, Pam, Melanie, and Vanessa.

And finally, the MOST IMPORTANT PERSON IN
MY LIFE...THE ENABLER OF ALL. To God, Jesus, and
the Holy Spirit...who have done immeasurably
more in me than I could ever imagine!

CONTENTS

INTRODUCTION

*I*f someone had told me as a teenager that I would one day write a book with a theme that centers on golf, I would have laughed out loud. Growing up in the foothills of South Carolina, my interests were elsewhere: winning the World Champion Clogging competition four years in a row, being crowned Miss South Carolina, an amazing experience at the Miss America pageant you will read about, and much more.

During those years, I never stepped my foot on a golf course—that didn't happen until after I was married. I still don't consider myself a golfer, but when our three children took up the sport with a passion, I spent hundreds of hours with them on courses and at competitive tournaments. Each received golf scholarships to Division 1 universities.

In the process, I began to see parallels between life on the links and the divine principles found in God's Word that lead to a life of significance.

If you're looking for tips on how to lower your golf score, try a book by Ben Hogan or Jack Nicklaus. But if you are ready to raise your *life* score, I am thrilled you have joined me on this journey.

Here is what you are about to discover as you take out your clubs on the *Front Nine:*

1. How to dream big and make your vision become a reality
2. As your DNA proves, there is no one in the universe just like you
3. The keys to building strong relationships
4. How your choices determine your future
5. The lessons you can learn from the "double bogeys" and mistakes of life
6. The secrets of dealing with adversity
7. How to build and strengthen your confidence
8. Steps to managing expectations
9. The amazing possibilities of your future

I am honored that you have allowed me to be your "caddy" and share what I have learned on the fairways and greens of the *Front Nine* of life.

– Sherry Bradshaw

TEE #1
DREAMS

I held my breath.

There I was, dressed in a rhinestone-studded evening gown weighing 20 pounds, anxiously standing on the stage of the historic Atlantic City Convention Hall—with over 21,000 faces before me. Millions more were glued to their TV sets watching the event unfold on the NBC Television Network.

It was Saturday night, September 15, 1985, and the moment had arrived for the crowning of Miss America 1986.

What a week! My face hurt from smiling. My body ached from spending every spare minute on a stationary bicycle, preparing to look as flawless as possible in that dreaded swimsuit competition. And on talent night, I gained new fans when I began clogging to the tune of "Are You From Dixie?"

It had all come down to this pivotal moment.

The handsome Gary Collins was the Master of Ceremonies. Most knew him from being a popular guest-star on dozens of television shows including *Hawaii Five-O, The Love Boat,* and *Charlie's Angels.* It was his fourth year hosting the Miss America Pageant.

When the top ten were announced, I was thrilled to hear

my name included. The next 90 minutes were a blur of hurried, intense activity to meet the demands of live television. The scores were thrown out (except for the judges' interviews) and the top ten began with another round of evening gown, swimsuit, and talent competition.

After the completion of the evening's competitions, the green light started flashing, alerting us that we were back on live TV. I found myself holding hands with the other finalists, wondering whose dream would come true.

Then Gary Collins began pacing back and forth on the stage, looking for words to ad-lib and fill the silence while the judges pondered their decision. The long wait was excruciating; time was passing in slow motion. Suddenly, a roving spotlight blinded my vision, and in seconds I was back into the moment.

After what seemed to be an eternity, the judges and auditors handed the bewildered host a card with the names of the five finalists.

I can still remember Collins saying, "I'm starting to get worried. Never in the history of this event has there ever been a tie for Miss America."

What? A tie? Standing awkwardly on stage, trying to hold a smile as the television camera panned the lineup of finalists, his words sent my emotions into a tailspin.

Collins began the countdown:

"The fourth runner-up is Angela Tower, Miss Alabama!"
"The third runner-up is Honey Castro, Miss Washington!"
"The second runner-up is Jonna Fitzgerald, Miss Texas!"

Somehow, I was still standing—but my knees were like limp, spaghetti noodles. What was written on the judges' card? Was I Miss America? Could my lifelong dream really become a reality?

A FRONT ROW SEAT

I discovered America in Westminster, a warm community of less than 3,000 in western South Carolina—located just a few miles from the Georgia state line. Other than the annual Apple Festival, there wasn't much excitement in town.

We lived in a ranch-style home built on a hill surrounded by grazing cattle—with the Appalachian mountains posed in the background like a picture postcard.

My father, Tom, had a road construction business, and my mom, Pat, who my sister and I affectionately called "The Rock," kept things running smooth on the homefront.

Growing up in a small town certainly has its advantages. When I was nine years old, we had a guest speaker at our church named Claudia Turner, the reigning Miss South Carolina.

Since there were no hotels in our town, the pastor asked

if she could stay with us. Not only was I mesmerized by her beauty, I was also drawn to her kindness and sweet spirit.

The next morning, at the Sunday service, I made sure I had a front row seat and listened spellbound to every word our house guest uttered. When Miss Turner stepped to the pulpit, she was holding her diamond-studded crown in her hands.

Even though I was young, I can still remember her passion as she said, "Let me tell you about something far greater than wearing the crown of Miss South Carolina. The most important title I have is being called a 'Child of the King.'" And she added:

"The crown I will be given in heaven one day will be more valuable than any presented here on earth."

Claudia's sincere words stirred within me the desire to give my life to Christ and have a personal relationship with Him. That memory-making day, I was forever changed. Not only did I invite Jesus into my heart and life, I desperately desired to share this Good News with others. Even before I knew what it meant, the Holy Spirit began to "do a good work in me."

Without question, being raised by Christian parents encouraged and enhanced my spiritual growth. I was blessed to be taught godly principles, which I saw exemplified every day. My mom and dad weren't perfect, yet their love for the

Lord permeated all aspects of our lives. They taught me God's Word and I was surrounded with a community that encouraged my Christian walk.

As I've flourished spiritually, the Author of my life has spent years working to perfect my faith—which is a work still in progress. One of my favorite passages from God's Word is found in Proverbs 3:5-6: "Trust in the Lord with all your heart, and lean not on your own understanding; in all your ways acknowledge Him, and He shall direct your paths."

Over the last four decades, I've probably done more leaning than understanding, but I rest in the assurance that "all things work together for good to those who love God, to those who are the called according to *His* purpose" (Romans 8:28).

THE BIRTH OF A DREAM

Not only was my heart changed the morning Miss South Carolina spoke in our church, but a dream was taking form within me that would grow to fruition.

In our neck of the woods, "clogging" was a big deal, and usually performed to country music. It's a type of folk dance in which the cloggers' tapshoes are used to rhythmically strike the heel, the toe, or both against a floor or each other to create a knee-slapping, toe-tapping, hand-clapping reaction from the audience.

I was all of ten years old when I was invited by Bill

Nichols, a clogging world champion, to join his newly-formed clogging team, "The Nicholodians." I was convinced that I could learn to dance and perform like he could. Bill was a phenomenal teacher and coach.

The long hours of rehearsals and competition paid off. At the official clogging conventions, our team won many titles, and I was fortunate enough to be named World Clogging Champion in the individual category four years in a row.

Evidently, competition was in my blood, and in 1980 I was named South Carolina's Junior Miss.

After high school, it was off to Clemson University—just a few miles down the road. Actually, no other college garnered even my slightest attention. I relished every minute of my time there and loved being a Tiger cheerleader for four years. I was overwhelmed and honored when named Homecoming Queen as a Junior.

Neither of my parents had the opportunity to attend college; therefore, my graduation in 1984 with a degree in Administrative Management was an especially proud moment for them. My dad hugged me and said, "An education is something no one can ever take from you, but it is drive and determination that will make you successful."

I have never forgotten the wisdom he shared with me on that day. I attribute much of my success to it.

The next year I clogged my way into the hearts of many at the Miss South Carolina pageant and won the crown. One of the judges was Donna Axum, a former Miss America from Arkansas.

The following months were hectic to say the least, being pulled in a dozen directions and offered endless advice on how to prepare for the Miss America contest—which I am very grateful for to this day.

"THERE SHE IS"

In Atlantic City, the week of the pageant was a whirlwind of non-stop rehearsals, wardrobe fittings, interviews with judges, and questions from the media.

From a lifetime of preparation, it all culminated in this final moment. My heart almost stopped as Gary Collins held the judges' decision in his hands and made the announcement: "The first runner-up is Sherry Thrift, Miss South Carolina. And the new Miss America for 1986 is Susan Akin, Miss Mississippi."

As the crowd cheered and flashes erupted, Collins began to sing the iconic song Bert Parkes had made famous years earlier, "There she is, Miss America. There she is, your ideal."

The dream I had anticipated coming true, and spent countless hours working toward, was over. I stood and watched another girl walk that ramp with my dream.

I later learned that when the judges voted there had actually been a tie, and I ended up with the short straw. Was I disappointed? Absolutely—*extremely* disappointed. Immediately fatigue, confusion, and shock set in because I had not allowed myself to think of the "what ifs."

I had been so laser-focused on being
Miss America that I never let my thoughts
entertain any other possibility. If doubts ever crept
in, I instantly kicked them to the curb.

It was my personal dream and no one else's—my decision, my work, and my life. Of course, there were numerous individuals who helped me along the way and I could not have gotten off the ground without their assistance and encouragement. But no one else could walk in my shoes—or dance, for that matter.

It took time to come to grips with my feelings and regroup, but looking back, I can see how God was guiding every step of my journey. When I returned to South Carolina, the welcoming arms of my faithful and loyal supporters were the perfect antidote for this sudden snakebite of defeat. The emptiness was temporarily filled with love and cheers as I explored new visions for my life.

The summer following the Atlantic City pageant brought another milestone. I married my college sweetheart, Bill Bradshaw. God has blessed us with three amazing children—Brewer, Thomas, and Collins. Please forgive a proud mother if I brag about them a little in this book.

YOUR DREAMS ROCK!

The last time I checked, life is all about living. When you

reach 50, you realize there is no Plan B, only Plan A—meaning the breath you are taking and the life you are living right now. It is impossible to reverse the sands of time and turn the hour glass upside down.

There is not a human being on earth who, alone with their thoughts, has not visited a field of dreams. Just look at the thousands who audition annually for *American Idol.* Yet there are millions more who never step out of their comfort zone. They let their dreams remain dreams.

What we envision gives us meaning and purpose. It creates hope, provides direction for our future, and sparks a desire within us to do more, be more, and *live!* In the words of Robert Schuller, "Daring to dream means daring to live."

Dreams stretch, challenge, and keep us from being stuck in the status quo and a life of mediocrity. I am a firm believer in the words of Jeremiah 29:11. God declared, "For I know the thoughts that I think toward you...thoughts of peace and not of evil, to give you a future and a hope."

Each of us were created with multiple purposes to fulfill and it is our job to seek our Creator's will in order to live an inspiring, significant, purposeful life.

The Lord never intended for His children to settle for average.

Most men and women store their dreams on a dusty shelf in a corner of their mind. My hope is that I can inspire you to blow the dust and cobwebs off of your unrealized dreams and actively seek to make them a reality. Always keep in the forefront of your mind that you never have a chance to win unless you play the game. It was only by signing up for the Miss America pageant that I had the opportunity to compete for the crown.

Let me offer these six vital steps:

One: Write Your Dreams Down

As simple as it may sound, physically writing your vision down on paper does something unique to your conscious mind. It allows you to see it with your eyes instead of focusing only on your thoughts. Doing this accomplishes two things: (1) it is an action step, and (2) it gives you a visual.

When you do this, it can be life-defining. The more detailed your dream is, the clearer and easier your path to follow becomes.

Two: Be Realistic

Let's be honest, gals. If you are 5'2" you probably won't take New York by storm as a runway model. But you could become a print model or do commercials. Or, if dogs head for the hills when you sing, you might want to rethink becoming a rock star. However, this doesn't mean you can't play an instrument or work in the music industry. Just be realistic about the gifts God has given you.

On the other hand, don't underestimate yourself. You can

have natural abilities as well as man-made ones achieved when you work extra hard in developing a skill. Both represent talent as you use and stretch your mind and physical body.

Since we are discussing dreams, why not let them be a little wild and out of the box? Remember, even the seed of a dream can germinate and produce a harvest.

> *Regardless of your background, upbringing, bank account, or who you know, dreams are personal and based on a God-given desire, talent, and interest.*

Ask yourself, "What do I excel at? What gifts do I have that come naturally to me?" I call these "strength zone" gifts.

Three: Do Your Homework

In this amazing age of information, you can stay in your home, research, and discover what successful individuals say helped them achieve their dreams and meet their goals. But in addition to researching, do your best to meet with men and women who have had great success; talk with them, ask questions, and observe them in action.

It is not important that they are famous or household names. There are many living around you who have realized their hopes and dreams, and there is much wisdom to be gleaned from their stories of achievement.

In addition, try to identify people who have accomplished

exactly what you envision doing—whether meeting with them personally, reading their story in a book, or Googling them.

For example, I read the story of a young man who was certainly no scholar in high school. Instead, he ran around with an 8mm camera shooting homemade movies—such as wrecks of his Lionel train set. The young man was even mistakenly placed in a learning disabled class. He was denied entrance to a film-making school, but while visiting Universal Studios, an executive, Chuck Silvers, met this kid, who was making 8mm movies, and invited him to come back sometime.

Well, the next morning, bright and early, dressed in a dark suit and tie, carrying his dad's briefcase (with nothing but a couple of candy bars inside) he gave a casual wave to the security guard who motioned him in. That entire summer, he was there every day, hanging out with writers and directors. Silvers smiled, but let him stay.

Ten years later, this "kid," now 28, directed *Jaws*, which made $460 million, then the highest-grossing movie ever. If you haven't guessed, I'm talking about Steven Spielburg.

Let stories like his inspire you.

Four: Create an Environment that Gives You the Best Chance to Reach Your Dreams

Take the time to read the story of Joseph, a man of many dreams, in the first book of the Bible. When this son of Jacob shared his dreams with his brothers, they became extremely jealous and angry. They even conspired to get rid of him. Of course, God's plan wasn't thwarted, but Joseph certainly endured hardship after vocalizing his dreams. He was sold into slavery in a foreign country and was falsely accused and sent to prison for attempted rape before realizing his dreams.

Let me encourage you to be careful with whom you share your vision for the future. Pick positive people who will water the seeds of desire within you. There will always be nay-sayers and those I call "dream vampires." Stay away from them or they will suck the life right out of your hopes and expectations.

Look for individuals who will lift you up and not crush your spirit. More than likely the encouragers will be those who are chasing their own endeavors and are anxious to run the race with you. I call them "dream angels"—their positive words arrive just at the right time. Make sure you enlist the best help possible. Ask yourself, "Do I have the right teacher?" Sometimes the best teacher is YOU!

Many people have been driven, yet had such few resources that they had to rely on their own ingenuity. As my dad always said, "They pulled themselves up by their bootstraps."

Five: Create a DMO—a Daily Method of Operation

What are you willing to do today to work toward your ultimate goal?

Each twenty-four hours may be different. I think about our three kids as they each competed at a high level in golf. Some days they played 18 holes, others they spent time on the driving range or working on their bunker shots. Then there were hours set aside strictly for putting and drills, while some days were totally dedicated to working on the mental side of golf. But every minute was purposed to take them one step closer to achieving success that would earn each of them a college scholarship in their sport.

Seconds add up to minutes, minutes to hours, hours to days, days to months, and months to years. They should not be wasted or squandered on trivial pursuits.

Achieving dreams takes time; you have to establish a plan and work it daily. The saying is so true: "Rome wasn't built in a day." It was built with a plan and a DMO.

If you journal or keep a calendar and write in it daily, this will lead to accomplishment. When you look back over a week and see your input, it does multiple things: it breeds confidence, creates good habits and work ethic, is a tool for measuring progress, and helps you make any necessary adjustments.

Six: Look for Opportunities

While surprises are possible, never expect opportunities to just drop out of the sky. While I was preparing for the Miss

South Carolina contest, my local pageant director and I would drive around the state, meeting random people and talking with them. The reasoning was to sharpen my communication skills and truly get a genuine feel of what it would be like to represent the state of South Carolina and its citizens. This opportunity was created: it didn't just automatically fall into my lap.

In golf, to emulate the pressure of what it is like to score in a tournament, our children rehearsed that too. At the end of a day of practice, they had a self-invoked rule that they couldn't leave the course until they made 10, ten-foot putts in a row. When they'd reach eight or nine, they would begin to experience the intense pressure you feel in a tournament when you need to make that putt for a birdie or to save par.

Sometimes opportunities that present themselves can be blessings in disguise. For example, you might be invited to attend a function or event on a day when you're bone tired and would prefer to put your feet up and stay at home. But, since you gave your word, you force yourself to be there because it's the right thing to do. In the course of the evening you meet an individual who shares something of value, contributing greatly to what you are currently working on. Or, you get an idea from someone about a direction in which you should be headed.

There are thousands of missed golden opportunities because we don't allow ourselves to look at things as just that—opportunities. Great ideas are nothing more than castles in the air unless they are carried to completion.

IT'S JUST THE BEGINNING

Now that you've finished the first hole, I pray you are well aware that my heart's desire is for you to have a heightened sense of the Creator and to realize that He wants you to dream big and work hard at making your vision become a reality.

As you progress to Tee #2, I trust you will understand your uniqueness; that no one in the universe is just like you—and your DNA authenticates this. Since the Master Craftsman designed you with a specific purpose in mind, it is time to fulfill His plan.

When you advance to Tee #3, you will discover the importance of building strong relationships and the value they bring to your life. While Tee #4 will stress the significance of our choices, no one should be deceived; our choices define us.

On Tee #5, we will examine how to analyze our mistakes and utilize the lessons learned, recognizing that *no* one can bypass the "mistake road" of life. As you play the 6th hole, you will find recommendations on handling adversity, which plays a role in everyone's journey. How you choose to embrace difficulties determines whether you produce good or bad fruit.

On Tee #7, we will look at the impact of confidence and how it can be built and strengthened. Playing the 8th hole, shows how we are to examine expectations and ultimately manage them.

Finally, on Tee #9, we will explore the amazing possibilities our lives hold.

Life on the Front Nine has blessed me with awesome adventures and taught me valuable lessons. I am so excited to have the privilege of sharing with you my loving heavenly Father and the things He has taught me!

Please, make wise use of what you are about to read as you perfect your game!

 ## NOTES FOR YOUR SCORECARD

- Dreams give you hope and direction for the future.
- God never intended for us to settle for average.
- Write your dreams down.
- Be realistic.
- Do your homework.
- Create a DMO—Daily Method of Operation.
- Look for opportunities.
- Carry your dreams to completion.

TEE #2
YOUR DNA

*W*hat an amazing person you are! At the time of your birth you were given a unique genetic code that determines your physical characteristics, your height, your voice, the color of your eyes, and so much more. This is called your DNA.

Where did it come from? Who placed it there? These tiny strands of biological data were imbedded in the first person ever created. God (Father, Son, and Holy Spirit) said, "Let Us make man in Our image, according to Our likeness" (Genesis 1:26).

Wow! Our DNA is there from the moment of conception. God created us exactly how He intended: "You are our Father; we are the clay, and You are our potter; and all we are the work of Your hand" (Isaiah 64:8).

Don't ever let Satan convince you that you aren't worthy; you are a child of God (John 1:12).

As we step up to Tee #2, here are some of the questions we will answer in this chapter:

- Is our DNA random, an accident, or the result of evolution?
- What is our true identity?
- Why were we created with the "free will" factor?

- How do we find our ultimate purpose?
- Why is receiving the "First Man" so important?
- The necessity of activating your spiritual DNA.

INTELLIGENT DESIGN

It is said that the amount of information contained in a single strand of human DNA would blow up *Wikipedia*—and this data contains a detailed, exact blueprint for the creation of a human being.

Bill Gates, the founder of Microsoft, stated, "DNA is like a software program, only much more complex than anything we've ever devised."

If you think this biological code wrote itself, you must be suffering from a mental deficiency (that is a polite way to say, "You're crazy!"). How could something as intricate as this have occurred from nothing or evolved from matter? It is absolutely impossible. Even today, man can only clone DNA, not create it.

The creation of this information requires *intelligence* far beyond the human mind—and God is the author of our DNA.

YOUR IDENTITY IS NOT IN YOUR GOLF SCORE

When our son, Brewer, started playing golf competitively, it was evident that his good and bad days depended on his golf score.

At first I didn't pay much attention to this because a lousy score prompted him to work harder. It was only when our second son, Thomas, started to compete in tournaments that we saw this attitude become a real problem. After all, the first thing someone asks following a round is, "What did you shoot?"

Not having played sports growing up, I initially deferred most of the guidance of athletics to my husband. Bill lettered in five sports in high school and played Division 1 college football, so he was accustomed to the ups and downs of athletics. Such know-how was foreign to me.

Then, when our daughter, Collins, entered the competitive scene in tournaments, the problem became so magnified that I knew something had to be done. Golf, as a sport and performance, was taking over our household.

We arranged for our three kids to sit down with a golf teacher and mentor, Curt Sanders. He talked to them about their identity in golf as it relates to them personally. We had been focusing on this regularly, but felt we needed to bring in someone outside the family who had succeeded at reaching their goal—to play golf at the collegiate level.

Curt, a Christ-follower and golf instructor, was an All-American at Ohio State and could speak their language. He talked to them about their identity being in Christ, and how in golf you lose more often than you win. He warned them about the danger of allowing their score to become their idol.

As a family, we spent many hours talking about how the sport should be seen as a vehicle to use and develop their

God-given abilities, not for themselves, but for their Maker.

Ephesians 2:10 provides first-class instruction on our true value. "For we are God's handiwork, created in Christ Jesus to do good works, which God prepared in advance for us to do."

Far too often we allow our identity to be revealed in other things. For women/girls, it may be wrapped up in how we look, the purse we carry, the shoes we wear, or how many "likes" we have on Facebook.

For men/boys it can often be the size of their paycheck, the make of their car, or the number of followers they have on Twitter. We can all fill in the blanks.

Society places far too much emphasis on "things" and performance—especially our *score*. But in the grand scheme of life, these don't matter. What counts most is the *reason* we chase these objectives. Is it for selfish gain and status, or for the glory of the Lord?

When a priest named Samuel was commissioned to choose the future king of Israel, he was guided to the house of Jesse. After interviewing the first of his eight sons, God told Samuel, "Do not look at his appearance or at his physical stature, because I have refused him. For the Lord does not see as man sees; for man looks at the outward appearance, but the Lord looks at the heart" (1 Samuel 16:7).

Finally, when young David was called in from tending his

flock of sheep, God said to Samuel, "Arise, anoint him; for this is the one!" (verse 12).

As a family we also know the Lord is examining our hearts. For this reason, we continually pray and turn the focus back to God, including where golf is concerned. It is an ongoing battle with plenty of lessons in humility. With wins have come media publicity, but so have high scores and forgettable tournaments. We also know what it's like to receive different treatment by others depending on whether our performance was superior or second-rate.

We need to mirror the reason for what we do to reflect Matthew 5:13: "You are the salt of the earth. But if the salt loses its saltiness, how can it be made salty again? It is no longer good for anything, except to be thrown out and trampled by man."

Be thankful that the Lord is using your skill to measure your "saltiness" and bring both His flavor and favor to those who cross your path.

THE "FREE WILL" FACTOR

From the beginning of time, God implanted the DNA of freedom and liberty in the heart and soul of man. It's called "free will." The Creator gave us the right to think, talk, and walk without the fear of being enslaved. Oh, there have been tyrants and political systems that have tried to control their subjects, but slavery goes against everything God stands for.

Can we abuse our free will? Of course. Adam and Eve are prime examples, and they paid a high price for their disobedience.

We are the captains of our own ship and can choose our destination—but the wise person lets God do the steering and set the course.

I thank the Lord for the liberty He has given us, yet we cannot impose our way of thinking on our neighbors. If we do we are violating *their* free will.

The gift of freedom the Creator gave us at birth is ours to keep—yet there are consequences for breaking both the laws of a government and the divine laws of heaven.

God did not send His Son to earth to *force* men and women to receive salvation. It is our choice to either accept or reject what Christ did for us on the cross. Jesus declared, "You shall know the truth, and the truth shall make you free" (John 8:32).

The next time you pull out a U.S. dollar bill from your pocket or purse, take a look at the phrase, "In God We Trust." It is evidence that our nation was established on biblical, godly principles. The Almighty was the focus of our Founding Father's intention and sacrifice.

Please ignore the "politically correct" textbooks that try to distort the true history of our nation. Our freedom is directly linked to our trust in God. The psalmist reminds us, "The

Lord's unfailing love surrounds the one who trusts in him" (Psalm 32:10 NIV).

Each of us has the free will to choose that trust.

How Do We Find Our Ultimate Purpose?

Whether you are running for a political office, attending grad school to become a medical doctor, or enrolled in a baseball camp trying to break into the pros, it's essential to stop and ask yourself, "What is my purpose for doing this?"

If you've never read Rick Warren's bestseller, *The Purpose Driven Life*, do yourself a favor and find a copy. Or, if you read it years ago, let me encourage you to read it again. You are probably at a different place in your life and the principles will apply to where you are right now.

I believe there is a holy God who created each person with an individual DNA and a unique purpose He expects them to fulfill.

You'll never convince me that we are born because of some random act, and "BOOM!"—here we are. As my friend Richard Mounce wrote on Facebook recently, thinking we just "happened" is like believing "an iPhone just washed up on the beach by itself and evolved!" No, it had a creator, and so do we.

The psalmist had it right:"For You formed my inward parts; You covered me in my mother's womb, I will praise

You, for I am fearfully and wonderfully made" (Psalm 139:13-14).

We have always asked our kids, "What is your purpose for playing golf?" The question is posed for a number of reasons, one being that we believe the objective has to be greater than themselves.

If our dreams are all about "me, myself, and I," we may reach those goals, but life at the pinnacle could be very meaningless and empty.

I believe all aspects of our existence are intertwined, and that connection is God driven! "For it is by grace you have been saved through faith, and that not of yourselves; it is the gift of God" (Ephesians 2:8).

Let me recommend a powerful book: *The Case for Christ*, by Lee Strobel. He was an award-winning journalist—and also an atheist—who set out to disprove his father's belief in God. After several years of inquiry, his eyes were opened, both rationally and spiritually, that Christ is divine. He experienced a marvelous conversion and now embraces the truth of Hebrews 11:6: "Without faith it is impossible to please Him, for he who comes to God must believe that He is, and that He is a rewarder of those who diligently seek Him."

No one is born without special talents and abilities which can be used by an all-powerful God to do purposeful things,

33

if we surrender, seek, and obey Him.

Even though we entered this world
with the imprint of God in every molecule of
every cell in our bodies, the enemy works
overtime to fill our minds with doubt.

If the Creator has placed a dream in your heart, bypass the devil's detour signs. Instead, consider them as part of a refining process to help us become more mature and complete (James 1).

I remember the day a challenge was given from the pulpit of our church. The pastor asked, "Who will stand and proclaim they will live for Christ?"

It didn't take but a few seconds before our middle son, Thomas, stood and publically acknowledged to the entire congregation that he would live for the Lord. Thomas became a Christian as a child, but this was a special moment of renewal for him.

It is a commitment every believer should make—whether they are asked to or not.

DISCOVER THE "FIRST MAN" IN YOUR LIFE

I make no bones about it—I'm a big football fan. As I have mentioned, I always root for my alma mater, Clemson University, where I was a cheerleader. As they say,"Once a cheerleader, always a cheerleader."

If you've ever watched a Texas A&M home football game on television, you'll hear the broadcasters talking about "The 12th Man"—the noise and cheers generated by the fans that can potentially spur on the team. At Kyle Field, just below the third deck, are the huge letters, "HOME OF THE 12TH MAN," a phrase that has been trademarked by the Aggies.

It's a concept that is also familiar in golf, where there is said to be a "15 club." Golfers are only allowed to have up to 14 clubs in their bag, so number 15 refers to the "mental game."

In our spiritual walk, Christ is not an extra, or an add-on, but the "First Man." He was there with God and the Holy Spirit at creation and present today to teach, comfort, encourage, protect, discipline, strengthen, and cheer for you.

I have been a Christian since I asked God's Son to come into my heart at the age of nine—and I can't imagine living without Christ.

I strongly believe that a life void of the First Man has no true purpose or meaning. And without meaning, we have no significance or hope. Remember, we are not here by happenstance; we were placed on this earth to fulfill a specific purpose. The Lord "chose us in Him before the foundation of the world" (Ephesians 1:4).

We only discover our reason for being when the First Man is our reference point. At the end of time, "each of us shall give account of himself to God" (Romans 14:12). Our works and actions will be tested by fire (1 Corinthians 3:13) and we won't be able to hide. The Lord knows the sincerity of our hearts, and the motives behind our actions.

John 3:16 best describes the First Man: "For God so loved the world that He gave His only begotten Son, that whoever believes in Him should not perish but have everlasting life."

If Christ is not Number One in all you do, there's no time like the present to make Him your top priority.

YOUR SPIRITUAL DNA

If you have strayed from the purpose for which you were born, there is a remedy. The blood of Jesus cleanses us, but it also does much more. It restores and activates the Father's DNA that resides in us. No longer do we have to use our own "will" in an effort to produce the fruit of the Spirit. Love, joy, peace, and other attributes will spring alive when His blood flows through us.

A man and a woman may be able to reproduce human life on earth, but only the Holy Spirit gives us new life that comes from heaven. At salvation, God breathed into our soul and gave us a spiritual rebirth. We already received our physical DNA from our parents, but now we possess the spiritual DNA from our heavenly Father.

This gives us an amazing distinction from the millions who have never been born again. We have new goals, attitudes, and values—and a desire to share Christ with others.

After our spiritual birth we are connected eternally to God in such a way that no matter what happens in our future, our heavenly genetic link to Him will not be broken.

Think about this. It has been proven by science that, because of its intricate structure, DNA cannot be totally removed or changed in an individual.

This is also true of our spiritual DNA. When we are reborn, our eternal union with God cannot be severed. Oh, we may rebel and try to go our own way, but this "spiritual genetic" connection remains. As Jesus said, "My sheep hear My voice;, and I know them, and they follow Me. And I give them eternal life, and they shall never perish; neither shall anyone snatch them out of My hand. My Father, who has given them to Me, is greater than all; and no one is able to snatch them out of My Father's hand" (John 10:27-29).

How awesome! Your DNA is not only yours on earth, but for eternity.

 ## NOTES FOR YOUR SCORECARD

- Your genetic code was placed in you by the Creator.
- Your identity must not be in your performance, but in your Maker.
- You were created with a free will, that must not be abused.

- Ask God to reveal the divine purpose for which you were placed on earth.
- You have been given special gifts, talents, and abilities that must never be wasted.
- Acknowledge and receive the "First Man" in your life.
- At salvation you are given your spiritual DNA which is yours for eternity.

Tee #3
Relationships

*A*s surely as the sun sets in the west, there will come a day when we will recognize that the most valuable things in life don't have a price tag, because they can't be bought; they can only be created.

Without question, our most meaningful memories will not be our homes, our cars, our bank accounts, nor trophies won; they will be the relationships we have with others. What will warm our hearts, invade our minds, and stir our emotions will be the moments that we have spent with the people we deeply care about—our relationships. They are measured by memories shared and time spent.

In this chapter we will discuss the importance of investing our time in others, how to stay in close communication with those we love, the qualities of a true friend, and the vital role of forgiveness in building relationships that last.

"Welcome to My World"

On an Easter weekend, more than a decade ago, two of our three children were playing in an American Junior Golf

Association event at the Chateau Elan in Georgia, just an hour away from where I grew up.

My parents came over to watch the kids play and spend the weekend. It always made for more fun when "Mimi and Papa" were present. Their lack of golf knowledge would make us all smile. Their innocent questions would be so funny at times that the kids would laugh hysterically. Of course my dad didn't care one bit.

After the round, he would attempt to play the par 3 course with the children. After hitting so many of their golf balls in the ponds, Dad would just say, "I was trying to feed the fish!"—and buy them a dozen more.

He just loved joining them in "their world," even if he had never been a golfer. All he experienced growing up was hard work in the logging and timber business. He and his eight brothers and sisters all pitched in to help the family financially. There were no extra hours for sports or childhood fun.

Over time, age caught up with my parents and they could no longer travel and watch their grandkids play golf. We all miss those days, but I wouldn't trade the memories and the lessons my parents provided for anything. Their presence in the lives of our children has been priceless.

Mom and Dad taught by their actions. They were living examples of the prayer found in Psalm 90:12: "Teach us to number our days, that we may gain a heart of wisdom." They treasured every hour spent with their children and grandchildren.

Whether or not you are familiar with the sport, instrument, hobby, or special interest of a young person, is an insignificant detail. It is the relationships and memories made that they remember.

This is how you forge a solid bond and have a strong voice in the life of a child.

At every possible opportunity, give your time to them. Get to know their friends and don't hesitate to travel to their home turf.

Even though they lived just over 100 miles away, Mimi and Papa packed their bags and happily ventured into our kids' world more times than I can ever count—birthday parties, sporting events, and school functions. It was a *priority* and we knew it.

I credit the close relationship that developed between our children and their grandparents to the "time investment" Mimi and Papa made. I have heard it said that "Love can be spelled T-I-M-E." And this has proved to be the cement in the bond between our children and their grandparents.

Even in her mid-seventies, my mom asked Collins to teach her to text. It took many hours before she mastered the art. Collins loved that she was willing to learn. I am most certain that our daughter will "play it forward" when she becomes a grandmother. But we all realize that communicating with family was that important to Mom. She didn't buy into the excuse, "I'm too old to learn." It was an act of love.

The words of King Solomon are
timeless: "Children's children are the crown
of the aged" (Proverbs 17:6).

Time is fleeting. Once it is gone it can never be recaptured.

STAY IN TOUCH

With today's ever-advancing technology, there is absolutely no excuse for failing to stay in close communication with loved ones and friends. Just as my mother made the effort to text, you have dozens of options at your fingertips.

I've learned to love *Snapchat.* It's an app you download on your smartphone. Then you send a picture of yourself or anything else along with a short message to a friend. What's amazing is that the image only lasts for about ten seconds, then disappears from your digital phone and is deleted from the company's server. More than 350 million photos are sent through this app every day.

Our kids forward me the funniest photos—what they had for breakfast, their sweaty bodies after an exhausting run, even a picture of their pay stub from a new job, or what they are reading in the Bible. I'm thrilled to be included in their day.

I recently had a friend from college move to Europe, and now, through social media, I am able to maintain our friendship and smile daily, keeping up with her exploits in London through *Snapchat.*

I realize that technology can be good or bad, depending on how we use it. For me, it helps foster relationships.

As a note of precaution. Never assume that what you say or send through a site like this is fool-proof. In fact, never put anything into cyberspace that you would be ashamed for the world to see.

Today, staying in touch is easier than ever. Gone are the days when land lines with tangled cords or pay telephones were the means of communication. It's a new day; take advantage of what's available. You can text, talk, Skype, or email at the touch of a button. Heck, I even go on vacation with my friends while sitting on my sofa at home when they post their pictures of trips on Facebook.

CHOOSE WISELY

Picking your friends is one of the most crucial and significant things you do. You don't get to choose your family, but it's awesome that you are able to select your friends. This is in no way a slam on family—by which I have been blessed. But I realize that for many individuals, "family" is not always associated with the word *awesome.* That's a tragedy!

We all have the freedom to choose, and since peer pressure can be intense, it's easy to become like those we associate with. It has been said, "Show me a man's friends and I will show you the man!" So we'd better make our selection with more than a casual thought.

I define a good friend as a person who is wise, loves, is loyal, encourages, sharpens, strengthens, and is full of energy. There is Scripture that highlights these characteristics:

- *Wise:* "Walk with the wise and become wise, for a companion of fools suffers harm" (Proverbs 13:20 NIV).
- *Loves, Loyal:* "A friend loves at all times" (Proverbs 17:17).
- *Encourages:* "A man who has friends must himself be friendly, but there is a friend who sticks closer than a brother," (Proverbs 18:24).
- *Sharpens:* "As iron sharpens iron, so a man sharpens the countenance of his friend" (Proverbs 27:17).
- *Strengthens:* "Two are better than one, because they have a good reward for their labor. For if they fall, one will pick up his companion" (Ecclesiastes 4:9-10).
- *Is Full of Energy:* "Keep away from any brother who is walking in idleness" (2 Thessalonians 3:6 ESV). The opposite of idle is active or full of energy.

I was taught that a friend is someone who is willing to get in the "trenches" with you. Our kids would say, "Someone who has your back." Surrounding yourself with the right people will help you grow stronger and wiser. In addition, it will offer you love in both the best and worst of times. And when trials come, you are guaranteed not to be alone.

Just like climbing aboard the wrong train and heading in a direction you don't want to go (as I did in New York recently), you can pick the wrong friends and wind up who knows where!

The Bible describes the kind of companions you certainly don't want to associate with:

- *The Wicked:* "The righteous should choose his friend carefully, for the way of the wicked leads them astray" (Proverbs 12:26).
- *The Angry:* "Do not make friends with a hot tempered person, do not associate with one easily angered, or you may learn their ways and get yourself ensnared" (Proverbs 22:24-25).
- *The Lazy:* We are to stay away from the idle, because, "If anyone will not work, neither shall he eat" (2Thessalonians 3:10).
- *The Drunkard or Glutton:* "Do not join those who drink too much wine or gorge themselves on meat, for drunkards and gluttons become poor, and drowsiness clothes them in rags" (Proverbs 23:20-21 NIV).

Thankfully, God's Word teaches us much more about choosing who we *should* surround ourselves with—and Who we should pattern our lives after, which is Christ.

It is clear that our objective must be to love and care for *all* people and be the light in a dark world.

Having a personal relationship with the Lord enables us to clearly see the dangers of taking the "wrong train." Choose your friends carefully and prayerfully.

A STRONG FOUNDATION

More than once I've been asked, "If you had to name the qualities and characteristics of a true friend, what would they be?

This is an easy one for me to answer. I only have to look at the loving mother who raised me. She has impacted every area of my life—the way I dress, the way I think, the way I parent, and especially how I embrace each day. She has been not just my mother, but my best friend.

It is written in Scripture, "The wise woman builds her house..." (Proverbs 14:1), and my mom did a wonderful job of constructing hers. The foundation was laid with the principle that "a happy heart makes the face cheerful" (Proverbs 15:13). She welcomed each day with joy, a song, and a smile.

While growing up, I was awakened most mornings to the sound of my mom singing to my sister and me a song based on Psalm 118. I will always remember the tune and the words:

This is the day the Lord has made,
Rejoice and be glad in it.
Whatever it brings, there's a song you can sing.
You may get tired, but don't fret.
Nature is yawning, a new day is dawning,
The sun will come shining through.
Is there a valley? We'll walk through it.
Climb a mountain? We can do it.
And I wish the top of the morning to you.

Just writing this brings tears to my eyes because it was the simple, ordinary things my parents did that had such a major influence on me. Her song inspired me to view my day with happiness and hope.

Then came the time when the tables turned. Mom reached the place where she could no longer take care of herself, and I found myself by her bedside, holding her hand and singing the same song: "This is the day the Lord has made...and I wish the top of the morning to you."

Even when she couldn't form a smile on her face, I could see the sparkle in her eyes.

After all these years, that song still shapes my day. What an incredible, lasting gift Mom gave me. I read this quote by Henry Ward Beecher, the 18th century clergyman: "What a mother sings in the cradle goes all the way to the coffin." Every word is permanently etched on our heart.

*I cannot over-emphasize how the simple,
inexpensive, positive things we do for our children or
others will have lasting, deep-rooted significance.*

Many individuals have a fascination with fame and applause, but the most important acts of our lives are done either quietly or anonymously.

When my mother became sick with a rare brain disease, the person my sister and I always called "the rock" would smile and say, "The rock is crumbling."

THE RIGHT STUFF

I remember a conversation she and I had several years ago after my aunt's funeral. The eulogies were emotional and beautiful and those who spoke shared about the hundreds of people my aunt's life had touched as a school teacher. On the way home my mom commented, "I don't think anyone would say those things about me."

It broke my heart to hear her words. I couldn't believe my mother would entertain such thoughts!

Although she never worked outside the home, inside she labored as hard as anyone I have ever known. Her quiet, serving example has been the paint on the canvas of my life for decades.

Shortly after mom became ill, my sister and I began to share the responsibility of going through our parents' mail and paying the bills. Never could I have imagined what I would learn about my mother in this stage of my life.

One day I opened a letter from a person in our past who was just a few years younger than me. It was from a woman named Judy, the youngest daughter of a man who worked for my father when I was young. He was uneducated, poor, and a bulldozer operator with a wife and four children.

I still remember the night my parents received a call that Judy's dad had shot and killed her mom in front of the children. My parents were devastated and beyond distraught. I can't recall many details because I was only nine, but I can still see Mom caring for the four children, taking them to the health department to get their vaccinations and doing all she could to help keep a sense of normalcy in their young lives.

Eventually, my folks were able to settle them into the Connie Maxwell Children's home in Greenwood, South Carolina.

Fast forward to the letter I read to my mom just recently. Judy wrote how much my parents meant to her, and expressed her sincere gratitude for the financial support Mom had provided to her and the family over the years. I knew as a young girl my parents had been involved, but now realize they had been loyal to her for a lifetime.

Her moving words spoke volumes to me about the unassuming, precious life my mother had lived out before me. It was the embodiment of what Christ taught: "But when you do a charitable deed, do not let your left hand know what your right hand is doing, that your charitable deed may be in secret; and your Father who sees in secret will Himself reward you openly" (Matthew 6:3-4).

When you go the extra mile for someone, it could be a fork in the road for that person. It sends a message of unselfishness and can make all the difference in their day, week, or life. That is an amazing characteristic of a friend.

The simple, careful, daily strokes of my mother's paint brush created a masterpiece. She represents well the words found in 2 Thessalonians 3:13: "But as for you...do not grow weary in doing good."

If you read Proverbs 31, it could have been written about her—especially verse 20: "She extends her hand to the poor, yes, she reaches out her hands to the needy."

I am convinced that in heaven my mother will be the equivalent of a "Rock Star."

Even if you think your actions are not needed
or appreciated, just remember, God sees—and
He is the only one who really matters.

The qualities that my mother has lived out loud in front of me, that of being positive, encouraging, kind, faithful, loyal, and giving, are the exact qualities that have made her my best friend.

THE FORGIVENESS FACTOR

Now comes the acid test of relationships. What happens when a close friend—even a member of your own family—treats you unfairly? Or what if you are the offender? I pray it never happens, but you will likely reach the point where a relationship is either on shaky ground or broken.

Years ago, I listened to an 18–hour tape series entitled "Growing Kids God's Way." The speaker was Gary Ezzo, a noted author and counselor.

One particular tape grabbed my attention, and I've never forgotten the message. The topic centered on forgiveness and humility and presented seven powerful words that can be the impetus for mending and healing broken relationships.

The words are: "I'm sorry. Will you please forgive me?"

Our words are hollow unless we follow through with our actions—giving a life lesson to our impressionable children.

All of us are imperfect people, parents included. We are wrong at times, and when this happens we should go to our children, own up to our mistake, and apologize. This is key for any parent, and it becomes very significant in all relationship building and communication.

Author Ezzo explained that most parents tend to think that acknowledging they are wrong is the equivalent of waving a white flag of surrender, giving into our kids and their whims—handing them more reasons not to listen to us. But he points out that children are smart and they model what we do. If we are unwilling to admit our errors, we are teaching them stubborn pride and a lack of humility.

We incorporated this teaching in our family and became more conscious and intentional at being quick to vocalize our mistakes—saying those seven powerful words, realizing we wanted our kids to grow up to become adults who would be vulnerable and admit their mistakes.

It would be very thrilling to see this implemented in educational settings, workplaces, friendships, marriages, and even churches.

Let's face it. We all have a hard time owning up to our faults, and saying, "I was wrong." Our ego rises up to the point that we almost stutter trying to release the words.

Scripture bluntly states, "God resists the proud, but gives grace to the humble" (James 4:6). And we know, "When pride comes, then comes shame, but with the humble is wisdom" (Proverbs 11:2).

Notice how grace and wisdom follow humility.

For me, it is a three step process. First, I say, "I'm sorry." Second, I ask for forgiveness. Third, I work to make sure I don't repeat the offense again.

In the vast majority of cases, the individual I have wronged is quick to forgive and has returned grace back to me. However, there have been times when I have sincerely apologized and was told I was forgiven—but I didn't *feel* that person's forgiveness. At that point the burden was off my shoulders. I had been totally obedient to what the Lord asked me to do—and if I was free in His eyes, that's what truly counts.

AN ACT OF THE WILL

I've learned that men and women are not as compassionate as God, and aren't as quick to forgive. Remember, the Lord knows the intent of our hearts and the depth of our sincerity. As we are told in Proverbs 16:2 (NIV), "All a person's ways seem pure to them, but motives are weighed by the Lord."

This verse brings me great comfort, because it reassures me that when I have erred and apologized, God sees the real me.

When you are wrong, humble yourself and be willing to say, "I'm sorry! Will you forgive me?"

Trust God in your humility! You can't control the other person's response but you will be rewarded for yours!

Regarding forgiveness, we cannot act on our emotions. As Corrie ten Boom stated, "Forgiveness is an act of the will, and the will can function regardless of the temperature of the heart."

Corrie's story has touched many lives. She was a Christian in Holland who was arrested and sent to a Nazi death camp for hiding Jews in her home during World War II. After her miraculous release, she practiced forgiveness and led a joyful life—even though she could never erase the horrific things she experienced and witnessed firsthand.

The reason God sent His Son to earth is so that we could have a personal relationship with Him. He expects us to demonstrate that same caring, compassion, and love to our family and friends.

 ## NOTES FOR YOUR SCORECARD

- Get out of your comfort zone and spend time in the world of your parents, your children, and your grandchildren.
- The hours you invest in people you love will pay dividends—here and hereafter.
- Communication is the glue of relationships. With today's technology there is no excuse.
- Choose your friends carefully and prayerfully.
- To have a friend, you need to be a friend.
- Make intentional, lasting memories with your family.
- Never grow weary in giving your best to others.
- Do good without seeking recognition.
- Be quick to admit your mistakes—even to your children and members of your family.
- Never be afraid to say, "I'm sorry. Will you forgive me?"
- First, seek a relationship with the Lord, then demonstrate His love to others.

TEE #4
CHOICES

*A*ccording to *Psychology Today*, the average person makes approximately 70 conscious, deliberate decisions every day—and hundreds more that are responses to our environment, such as turning the car's steering wheel to stay in our lane.

On the pages that follow, I want to share what I have learned concerning making choices, including the importance of trusting wise counsel, preparing for the results of decisions which have both negative and positive outcomes, and the role of visualizing success.

In addition, we will discuss how God uses "all things" for our good, how right choices lead to a bountiful harvest, why we need to choose a testimony over a title, the necessity of investing in the lives of others, and why we must decide to live a life of significance.

OVERCOMING A MAJOR "GUT WAR"

Let's begin with the issue of choosing wise counsel. People who know me well understand that I have never liked to fly. Airports and airplanes have always given me a "gut war." Butterflies, nerves, anxiety, fear, or whatever you want to label it, find their way to the pit of my stomach.

If you were a stranger seated next to me on the plane, you would probably be my "new best friend" by the time we landed!

This has been an ongoing battle I have been fighting for years. When there are unusual noises or turbulence, my natural reaction is to grab the person sitting close by, clutch their arm and bury my head in their shoulder. It doesn't matter if I know them or not. Pride immediately flies out the window!

A few years ago I discovered that our children argued over who had to sit next to me when we were flying as a family. Even Bill is in the mix of letting the children share the burden of baby-sitting their mother in the air.

Once on board, fear creeps in and keeps me company. I've tried sleeping, spent time in prayer, and read my Bible to help calm my frayed nerves.

I found very little victory over this ongoing problem until one particular flight. I was heading to a golf tournament by myself and the Lord placed an off-duty pilot right beside me. The takeoff was uneventful until about 45 minutes later when we experienced major turbulence. I felt as if I were free-falling as the plane bounced in the sky like a rubber ball. Just imagine the surprise of the seasoned pilot who was drinking his coffee and enjoying the paper, when all of a sudden I grabbed his arm, holding on for dear life!

Thankfully, he was an angel. For the next two hours, he patiently talked me through my unjustified and over-the-top fears.

The pilot was gracious, understanding and, not to mention, knowledgeable on how to deal with people like me. In simple terms, he explained air pockets, weather streams, required precautions, and all the measures that are taken to ensure safety.

The more he shared, the more insight I gained, all the while feeling a release from the fear that had held me in its grips for so long.

Later, as I read the words of King Solomon, they certainly fit this situation: "A wise man is strong, and a man of knowledge increases power. For by wise guidance you will wage war, and in abundance of counselors there is victory" (Proverbs 24:5-6 NASB).

I was afraid because I lacked knowledge and understanding, and was in a war with my anxiety. God used that pilot (a stranger, but who I now call a counselor) to be a blessing in my life.

I still have the habit of grabbing someone by the arm when unexpected bumps pop up during flights, but I don't have the same trepidation driving to an airport or the sleepless night before the trip that I once faced.

Fear can paralyze anyone. It is a tool of the enemy to keep us trapped in quicksand and prevent us from moving forward or making a decision. It's not a fun place to live— and we usually don't thrive there.

A huge learning curve for me was how to confront the fear of the unknown in a given circumstance. I now trust the wise counsel from individuals who have more expertise than me regarding the situation. It definitely increases my strength and power and, many times, allows me to win the mini-wars, and often *major* wars of life!

Many are held back from being all God created them to be because of a lack of courage. And the antonym for courage is fear—which needs to be greatly reduced in our lives.

To achieve worthwhile accomplishments, we have to make the decision to not just exist as a "warm body"—we need to be a "*hot* body." I believe wholeheartedly that every man, woman, and child has a created purpose. There are specific things each of us are designed to do, not just to take up space on earth.

So to grow without the pressure of fear, I have learned that choosing to seek wise counsel and a desire to be *teachable* is extremely beneficial.

THE OUTCOME

Our lives are defined by our choices—big and small. And

they can all lead to positive or negative outcomes.

Seemingly insignificant decisions can bring disastrous results. There are times we choose options that seem harmless, but if repeated they can layer into bad habits that have horrible consequences. It's like driving and not seeing a dead end, or ignoring the guardrails that are there to keep us from veering too far left or right.

For example, we often give little thought to what we choose to eat, but our choices really affect us. Take a 12-year-old girl who may enjoy one harmless Krispy Kreme donut. All of a sudden, her tastebuds are out of control and that one innocent treat leads to another and another, which affects her weight. Next creeps in low self-esteem from packing on the pounds and not being picked to be a cheerleader because she is too heavy.

Or how about a teenager or college student who decides to take a drink of alcohol. Most studies show that young teens make such a choice as a way to fit in and be part of their peer group. If they have a drink they are "in." The alcohol and its affects lowers their inhibitions and they feel they can talk to the opposite sex with "liquid courage."

This is definitely the wrong motivation for drinking. Ask any drug addict, "What was your first drug?" Almost always, they will answer, "Alcohol." It is the doorway to all other drugs.

Our biological makeups all vary and no one can tell when a first or second drink will trigger an eventual addiction, either to alcohol or something worse.

I am not lecturing about alcohol, but more times than not it has negative consequences. No one takes a first drink intending to become an alcoholic, be ticketed with a DUI, or say and do things under the influence that they would have never done otherwise.

There are also choices that have very *positive* outcomes. For example, you can decide to own your own faith when you go to college. As a young person you were raised to attend a house of worship, but when you move out of the home and arrive on campus, it is often a time of "finding out who you are."

You're free! You don't have to go to church on Sunday because you are living independently, but you choose to. You take it a step further and join a small group to get involved. You find that you love the fellowship, the friendships, the encouragement. This results in building strong relationships that offer much needed support in your college years when there are often struggles. By making this choice, you also have access to adult leadership and mentorship.

Perhaps you are a freshman and you have heard about the "freshman 15"—referring to added pounds. Determined not to be a part of that number, you intentionally choose to exercise the first day of college and make it a daily pattern. Your plan pays off. At the end of your freshman year, your clothes still fit, and you still weigh the same as when you started.

*Choices are roads. Some can lead you to a
pot of gold; others to the edge of a blind cliff.
This is why the path you take is so vital.*

THE POWER OF VISUALIZATION

There are times when, no matter how hard we try, we can't see what lies ahead. However, we can make the choice to stop, think, and visualize what we are about to do.

When our son, Brewer, was a freshman at Clemson University and a member of the golf team, his wise and helpful teammate, Kyle Stanley, told him repeatedly, "You've got to see the shot way before you hit it!"

That's when I started paying attention to the word "visualization."

Kyle talked about seeing every shot perfectly to the point of thinking about the distance and what club he would pull for each one. But most importantly, Kyle would visualize the perfect shot in his mind's eye and go through all 18 holes. He would see every stroke, even putting and chipping. Going through this process was a discipline Kyle developed as he competed at a high level in golf and later in PGA tournaments.

This so resonated with Brewer that even when he was not at the golf club, he could play the entire course in his head.

What you allow yourself to think or visualize mentally is

a form of seeing. For example, our middle son, Thomas, talked about spending extra time on the golf range in order to see "a positive" ball flight. He spent hours imprinting the "good stuff" in his mind, then to his eyes, and finally to his physical body.

The power of the mind is written about in the Bible. It speaks of taking "every thought captive" (2 Corinthians 10:5), which applies to so many areas of life.

"THINK ON THESE THINGS"

Developments in science and sports validate what Scripture teaches us about the workings of the mind. How we think powerfully impacts our future. As Paul the Apostle wrote, "Finally, brothers and sisters, whatever is true, whatever is noble, whatever is right, whatever is pure, whatever is lovely, whatever is admirable—if anything is excellent or praise worthy—think about such things" (Philippians 4:8 NIV).

Paul continues with this encouragement: "Whatever you have learned or received or heard from me, or seen in me—put it into practice. And the God of peace will be with you" (verse 9).

Remember, he is speaking about the power of what we think—but we cannot accomplish these things in our own strength. We need the omnipotent, all-knowing God who sees our past, present, and future.

Too often we limit our lives to what we know and view in the moment. Our thoughts tell us this is what we should trust.

You can have faith or you can have complete control, but you can't have both.

If you want God to do something off the chart, learn to take your hands off the steering wheel. Give Him your mind and allow Him to empower and enable you to do much more than your thoughts can ever drum up.

I am not implying you can "positive think" your way to success and a life of fulfilled dreams. The Almighty is not to be used as a "Genie in a Bottle" to make all our wishes come true. God gave you a mind and specific instructions on how to use it. He is divine and has a divine plan—and desires to fill our days on earth with purpose beyond what we can comprehend.

He is saying to you and me: "For my thoughts are not your thoughts, nor are your ways My ways" (Isaiah 55:8).

The greater our faith the more we can see His supernatural power at work. "For who knows a person's thoughts except their own spirit within them? In the same way no one knows the thoughts of God except the Spirit of God" (1 Corinthians 2:11 NIV).

Just like visualizing in golf, accepting Christ allows the Holy Spirit to enable you to "see" the amazing things God can and will do in and through you. Paul reminds us to, "put it into practice." This action step is our decision. The Lord is then given the freedom to imprint Himself and paint a picture beyond our wildest dreams.

MUD BALLS AND DIVOTS

Another place where we are faced with choices is on the golf course. Let me point out a situation where your decision can make you either grumble and complain, or develop and mature.

There are many variables in the sport. Two lurking vampires that golfers dread to see, especially in a tournament, are "mud balls" and those that land in "divots." I've seen players execute a great shot, only to walk up and face either of these game-stealers. You can often see the joy, peace, patience, kindness, and self-control drain right out of them on the spot!

It's a good feeling to hit the middle of the fairway, but your heart sinks when you find your ball in a divot, swimming in mud, resulting from rain the night before.

The rule in these situations is to "play it down" (meaning you can't pick up your ball and clean it). For non-golfing readers, a divot refers to the scarred area in the fairway, sometimes up to an inch deep, that's left when turf is dislodged from hitting a shot.

When this happens, it can affect your ball flight and direction on the next shot. The same applies to a mud ball.

While caddying, I have witnessed this first-hand. To say the least, it is very frustrating (and unfair). Over the years, after watching countless rounds of golf, I have learned that whether pro or amateur, no one is exempt from these unlucky shots. It happens to everyone.

GROWING PAINS

As in golf, so it is in life; everyone faces unfairness. We may work very hard to control our circumstances, but the unexpected can crop up at any time and rob us of the payoff.

I have learned from personal experience that God can use these difficult situations to cultivate healthy fruit—especially the fruit of patience and self-control.

> *Again and again I've seen how*
> *the Lord uses "all things" to work for good*
> *for those who love Him and are called*
> *according to His purpose.*

For this spectating mom of three golfers, there have been thousands of challenging opportunities, exposing the strengths and weaknesses of our family in living out what the Bible calls "the fruit of the Spirit."

Paul the Apostle tells us, "But the fruit of the Spirit is love, joy, peace, longsuffering, kindness, goodness, faithfulness,

65

gentleness, self-control. Against such there is no law" (Galatians 5:22-23).

I don't think there is a golfer, or parent of a golfer, alive who would deny the obvious benefits of these attributes. God has used this particular sport to continually refine our family. I strongly believe in the truth found in this passage and try to live accordingly. It is a measuring stick that teaches us how to grow and gain wisdom to handle every obstacle that arises.

Our heavenly Father's first and foremost priority is to help us grow deeper and richer in our intimate relationship with Him, even if this means traveling down the lonely road called "Unfair."

We all need to possess the quality called patience, but it is often developed best through adverse circumstances.

Allow me to mention Joseph again, a young man who was sold into Egyptian slavery. God used extreme injustice, jealousy, prison, false accusations, and alienation to develop and prepare him to be mature enough to forgive—and eventually save hundreds of lives, including the lives of his own family.

Mud balls and divots can either cause you to moan and be dejected, or mature and develop. It's your choice.

TWO COACHES

The next decision I want to address concerns what kind of seed we are planting for our future.

Two of my all-time favorite coaches and authors are football's Tony Dungy and basketball's John Wooden. Their lives have profoundly impacted thousands and both have a legacy of making wise choices.

Each has reaped an abundance of success, but more important, a bountiful harvest of significance. I love reading their books because of the "fruit" produced from their lives.

Coach Wooden is quoted as saying, "Be more concerned with your character than your reputation, because your character is what you really are, while your reputation is merely what others think you are."

There is a huge difference. This is why we need to take an introspective look at ourselves, to make sure what we have on the inside are qualities worth sharing with others.

In the words of Coach Dungy," It's about the journey—mine and yours—and the lives we can touch, the legacy we can leave, and the world we can change for the better."

When their former players and assistants speak of them, the one thing they both have in common is that their actions are synonymous with their words. They are committed to living out biblical principles and have sown good seed.

These words of Scripture still hold true today: "Do not be

deceived, God is not mocked; for whatever a man sows, that he will also reap" (Galatians 6:7).

You and I become the sum total of our choices. I've heard it said, "with age comes wisdom." But I believe this is only true if we take our past experiences, and those of others, and learn from them. We must embrace these lessons—and any feedback we receive—and apply them in our future decisions and actions.

Over and over I have experienced the "sowing and reaping" principle established in God's Word and watched it lived out hundreds of times—some for the greater good and some leading to a spiraling downfall.

How much better to make the right choices and reap the same type harvest as men like Tony Dungy and John Wooden than face the alternative.

TITLES OR TESTIMONIES?

As you prepare for a time of reaping, there are many decisions you will need to make: one involves the input you need to plant in your heart soul and mind.

I have become much more of a bookworm in the past few years because of one of John Wooden's quotes. He said, "If you chose not to become a reader, you are choosing to live a life of ignorance."

Wow! That really resonated with me, so I increased my reading time.

I had to search, but I finally found and re-read a book written by Tony Campolo that I had enjoyed years ago. His wisdom in *Who Switched the Price Tags?* strongly influenced me then and today, and has reinforced many of my convictions—one being to answer the question whether our lives are lived for "Titles or Testimonies?"

On my first go-around with this book I was in my twenties, having recently relinquished the title of Miss South Carolina. His words made me take a step back and examine how I would live the rest of my life. Having been a title holder and a representative of our state, I felt a huge responsibility to be a positive role model, respectful of the position with which I had been entrusted.

I also found myself reevaluating my role as a Christian. How well do I represent Christ? Is it a drudgery, or a delight? Do I give back to God out of a thankful heart? Do I invest my time in those who have yet to believe?

Tony Campolo's book spells out the importance of a life well lived. He emphasizes over and over again that we often lead such absorbed, preoccupied lives that we "switch the price tags" on what is of true value. He poses the question, "How would we want to be remembered?"

At our funeral, do we want a long list of accolades and accomplishments read or a long list of lives in whom we have positively invested?

69

My trophies and titles have been rewarding, but I would much rather choose the lives! The one thing money can't buy and death can't take away is the people we value and have taken the time to positively affect.

BEYOND THE CRISIS

Most men and women don't give much thought to death, unless they are sick or lose a loved one. The choices we make in this area are so meaningful.

When my mind thinks on this topic, I immediately remember Dawn Smith Jordan who was also a title holder. I passed on the crown of being Miss South Carolina to her in 1986. What a privilege to transfer the silver, jeweled tiara to a woman who has used her title to take a powerful testimony all over the world.

Dawn's story is best told by her, but let me share the highlights. While in high school, her sister, Sherrie, was kidnaped from their driveway in Lexington, South Carolina, and was later found murdered. The account of the horrific way that Sherrie died and all the details that Dawn and her family endured are so tragic and unfathomable that it was the subject of a motion picture.

Dawn's book, *Grace So Amazing,* has encouraged me to see how someone like her has risen above such a tragedy, yet with God's help, has turned this utter darkness into light.

I trust you will never have a story like Dawn's, but

nothing should keep you from a testimony of having the right "price tags" in life. We must never allow a crisis to sidetrack us from human kindness: sending a card or email to encourage someone, or forfeiting a vacation to go on a missions trip. Perhaps you can spend a Thanksgiving Day feeding the homeless, or simply taking a meal to a sick neighbor.

It's ironic how the more we step "outside of ourselves" and invest in someone else, the more we have the opportunity and privilege to increase our "price tag" or what I call, "our testimony."

THE SIGNIFICANCE FACTOR

Now let me tell you about a choice you have to make that is yours alone. It involves one of the most thought-provoking questions you will ever ask yourself: "Am I living a life of significance?"

Have you ever felt as if your daily routine is so mundane and monotonous, or so busy that you hardly have time to stop and and catch your breath? If you have children, no matter the age, you can definitely relate to the unexpected mess and craziness that life can throw your way. Things can get so hectic that paying attention to yourself and your needs are not just on the back burner; they are kicked out the back door!

Of course, there are responsibilities we must fulfill such as school, job, volunteer positions, church, being a parent or a spouse, etc. However, the significance I am referring to is personal—taking the time to care for yourself and knowing God's plan for you *daily!*

Please pay attention to this powerful counsel: "Above all else, guard your heart, for everything you do flows from it" (Proverbs 4:23 NIV).

God wants us to take the time to look after ourselves—to protect our heart so that what we do on a daily basis can have meaning and purpose. The verse doesn't say this affects only some things, but *"everything we do!"*

Learning what that really meant has been a fork in the road for me. I now have a better understanding of the words found in Mark 12:30-31: "'You shall love the Lord your God with all your heart, with all your soul, with all your mind, and with all your strength.' This is the first commandment. And the second, like it, is this: 'You shall love your neighbor as yourself.'"

As I will explain in a moment, I got this a little wrong. No, *I got it a lot wrong!*

> *Sometimes we can have great*
> *intentions, but moving down the road*
> *of life we suddenly have a "blow out" and*
> *realize, "Wow, I didn't expect that!"*

Even if we are well-meaning, God loves us so much that He will do anything to reel us in and love us back to a place of grace, restoration, peace, and rest.

My "blow out" occurred when I reversed verses 30 and 31. I got things backwards! I started to love neighbors more than God! This was in the form of "people pleasing!"—a psychological term you hear quite often referred to as "enabling."

First, the definition of *neighbor* can mean anyone—your kids, your husband, your mother or father, your brother or sister, extended family, friends, the person next door, co-worker; you fill in the blank. Your neighbor is anyone but yourself. The act of working to help, encourage, or please, can become an "idol"—especially if it takes precedence over God.

What does putting the Lord first and applying verse 30 truly mean? First, it involves having a daily quiet time with your heavenly Father and opening your *heart* to Him. This time alone is key to "guarding your heart" and allowing *Him* to direct your every move and daily schedule. God wants everything from you personally— your heart, soul, mind, and strength. *After* that comes everyone else.

If this gets reversed, you are headed for trouble. Again, your significance starts with Mark 12:30, not verse 31. That comes second.

Yes, we must choose to look after ourselves, so we will have the strength to look after others.

FIRST THINGS FIRST

The decisions you make regarding your priorities will have an ever-increasing impact on you—and the world around you.

Everyone has responsibilities that have to be fulfilled on a daily basis. Sometimes, if you are "prone to please" like I was, you can think that making sure everything gets done is pleasing to God. It is. But this is the murky, grey area that was *soooo* backwards in my life. I enjoyed making everything work for everyone, keeping peace and life running smoothly! Some years ago, I even had a part-time personal assistant in our home comment, "Wow, you are all things to all people. I don't know how you do it."

I did it all well for awhile until the exhaustion and emptiness set in. I would hit the floor in the morning, "suit up for the day," charge forward, and handle any upheaval that came my way, even if it wasn't my problem, but one I created!

I made myself way too responsible for others. After all, wasn't I "loving my neighbor"? Of course. But what I wasn't doing was guarding my heart—presenting my day to the Lord and inviting Him to see when I needed to "catch the ball" or when I needed to "let it drop."

Figuring out my priorities in life and where the line

needed to be drawn was only found in taking the matter to the Lord.

I came to the ultimate realization that I was not my brother's keeper for some of the things I was owning. I was even taking ownership for someone else's bad day!

Then God started revealing His plan for my daily life and showed me where I was taking on things that were not mine. I was actually robbing another person of their responsibility! This was eye-opening to me!

Catching balls that were thrown in the air by others eventually reached the place where I was running, stretching, and jumping so fast that I hit a wall. Something had to give!

If this sounds familiar to your own situation, please stop what you are doing and ask the Lord to show you how to "drop your hands." Ask Him about your significance and how He sees your responsibility.

When you sincerely seek the Lord with all your heart, soul, mind, and strength, He will show up and I can guarantee that you won't be disappointed. A few minutes of His presence changes everything.

God will help you navigate through life, organize your hours, and let you know specifically what He has purposed just for you.

The choice is yours.

NOTES FOR YOUR SCORECARD

- In making decisions, trust wise counsel.
- Prepare for the results of choices that can be either positive or negative.
- Choose to visualize a successful outcome.
- It's your decision to either complain or mature.
- God uses "all things" for our good.
- Right choices lead to a ripe harvest.
- Always choose a testimony over a title.
- Make a decision to invest in the lives of others.
- Guard your heart—everything you do comes from it.
- Choose to live a life of significance.

Tee #5
Mistakes

*I*f you're searching for common ground with others, you don't have to look far. We all make mistakes. The difference is in how we handle them.

Some face their errors head on, take full responsibility, and learn from them, while others either ignore, repeat, or put on a "coat of pride"—unwilling to admit what caused the blunder.

Most people know how to get up when they fall—that's how as toddlers we learned to walk. So take heart; mistakes can be "teachable moments" we not only overcome, but which eventually allow us to pick up speed and run!

On this fifth tee, we will look at (1) the mistakes we make with our words, (2) what to do when someone offends us, (3) self-inflicted wounds caused by the wrong first impression, (4) the dangers of over-extending ourselves, (5) how jealousy and envy can torpedo our success, and (6) what we can do to avoid duplicating the same old mistakes.

Double Bogeys

To a person playing golf, double bogeys are a nightmare.

It means you hit two shots over par on any given hole. It is hard to make up ground in your score when this happens.

In this journey called life, I've figuratively experienced many double bogeys, and would like to share one in hopes that you will have a better score when you reach the "Back 9" of your walk.

The only word I can think of to describe a double bogey is UGLY! A pro would tell you this reveals a need to work on your short game, but off the course it has happened to me when I found myself, "not holding my tongue." More than once I have been guilty of violating the famous quote, "If you can't say something good about someone, don't say anything at all." Any way I slice it, that's one of my deep regrets.

Of course, I could justify my actions and make you think I had reasonable cause in some cases. But looking back, I wish I could be the person about whom others would say, "She never said anything bad about anyone!"

Words can hurt; they can be sharp and cut to the core, and they have certainly wounded me deeply at times. As I have taken a close look at this area of my life, I realize that for as much as I have been wounded, I have also injured others (killed them with my words). So yes, you could say I am a murderer. But with God's help, I have asked forgiveness and am now trying to purposely think of the consequences of my words before I speak.

Some practical ways I am working to overcome the dreaded "doubles" is to navigate the "fairways and greens" with Scripture. For example, Jesus tells us, "For every idle word men may speak, they will give account of it in the day of judgment" (Matthew 12:36). Yikes!

We are also told, "The tongue...is a fire, a world of evil among the parts of the body. The tongue is so set among our members that it defiles the whole body, and sets on fire the course of nature; and it is set on fire by hell" (James 3:6).

There are many other verses that speak to this issue, but this is all it takes for me to wish I could cram a sock in my mouth at times!

A word, once it leaves your lips,
can never be taken back.

Here are a few tips that can help you achieve a better score:

1. *Being Silent:* Silence can never be misquoted and is also a powerful form of communication. "Whoever guards his mouth and tongue keeps his soul from troubles" (Proverbs 21:23).
2. *Asking for forgiveness:* With a sincere heart, speak to the person you have offended.
3. *Praying:* Ask God for "self control," which is a fruit of the Spirit.
4. *Confronting:* A righteous anger can be used in a positive way to give you courage. Be sure to choose your words wisely.

5. *Letting go:* Once you address the issue, bury it in the sea of forgetfulness.

6. *Realizing that everything starts with the heart:* "For out of the abundance of the heart [the] mouth speaks" (Luke 6:45). That's where it all begins.

Just as golfers work tirelessly on their "short game," we must allow the Lord to "do a good work in us" and change our hearts. A natural byproduct will be that our conversations will take on a new vocabulary worthy of our character. It will help us eliminate mistakes—especially those ugly doubles!

"TWO WRONGS DON'T MAKE A RIGHT!"

Double bogeys can creep up in the most unexpected places. They are especially harmful if we don't know how to respond when someone offends us. This was a lesson I learned as a young girl.

Growing up, when I was angry with my sister or felt wronged by someone else, the first words to fly out of my dad's mouth were, "Remember, two wrongs don't make a right!" If I heard this once, I heard it a thousand times.

My father was teaching a biblical principle: "Do not repay evil with evil or insult with insult. On the contrary, repay evil with blessing, because to this you were called so that you may inherit a blessing" (1 Peter 3:9 NIV).

As a young girl, avoiding this trap was very hard to do and, as an adult it is still difficult. This is a divine truth that needs to be reinforced in today's get-even world. Now that our children are young adults, I talk about this whenever the opportunity arises and intentionally do my best to demonstrate it through my actions. It's what I like to call, "living out loud!"

As Christians, we must follow the example of our heavenly Father, forgiving wrongs and not seeking revenge when someone offends us. Yet we must look at the context of each situation and be willing to "confront" in an appropriate manner when a wrong occurs—making sure we are not doing so purely out of revenge.

For example, when our kids were playing in golf tournaments, at times they would come home mad and frustrated over someone cheating on the course. Usually, they kept their mouths shut when this occurred, but I believed it was their responsibility to address (but not falsely accuse) the wrong.

Golf is called "a gentlemen's game," but if you are in a group where cheating is taking place, it is your obligation to protect the integrity of the field.

In addition, we can't turn a blind eye at cheating in school. I'm not implying that my kids are perfect angels. If we are truly honest, we are *all* guilty of committing wrongs that need to be corrected.

We run away from this truth either because (A) we don't want to shine the light on our own sins, (B) we simply do not have the courage to confront, or (C) we fear what others may say or think. So we bite out tongues and remain silent.

*When we see a wrong, we have
a duty to pray and bring the situation
out in the open <u>appropriately</u>.*

Let me emphasize that we can be sincere, yet sincerely wrong about our approach.

Whatever the case may be, we must not wear blinders as if nothing took place. We usually find that those who wound us "are darkened in their understanding and separated from the life of God because of the ignorance that is in them due to the hardening of their hearts" (Ephesians 4:18 NIV).

I have used these words to help our children understand that some individuals, when shown the error of their ways, are unwilling to admit their mistakes or that they are wrong.

Again, our only responsibility is to point out the error, not belabor the problem. In His timing, the Lord will do the rest. It is "God who will render to each one according to his deeds" (Romans 2:6). Sometimes on the Front Nine—more often than not—when I drop my hands and surrender, leaving it up to God, I see justice served. I don't wait on it or look for it. I simply move on. The old saying is true: "What comes around, goes around!"

We are not held accountable for, nor can we control, anyone's behavior but our own. However, we must practice forgiveness and pray daily for our offender. As it is written, "Love your enemies and pray for those who persecute you" (Matthew 5:44).

This is often easier said than done, but we are required to do so and not go AWOL. The reassuring part is that we don't have to face these challenges in our own strength. We have help and comfort from above: "But whoever looks intently into the perfect law that gives freedom, and continues in it—not forgetting what they have heard, but doing it—they will be blessed in what they do" (James 1:25 NIV).

Another nugget of truth my dad impressed upon me is: "If you are in the 'majority' in your behavior, you'd better take another look. I find that people in the 'minority' are often the ones doing the right thing."

When we are wronged, our natural human tendency (majority) is to seek to get even. It's much tougher to confront when necessary (minority) and trust God with the outcome —even if you don't immediately see the desired results in the other person.

Most people aren't willing to do the "hard right thing" because it takes them away from the popular crowd. But I believe you will find the courage and determination to call "right right" and "wrong wrong"—and gain true friends in the process.

FIRST IMPRESSIONS

We've been looking at how to respond when we've been

wronged, but some of the greatest mistakes being made are our own.

As many parents are learning the hard way, there are errors that need correcting under their own roof.

For example, every few days, we read another story about young people who are making tragic mistakes by posting inappropriate pictures on social media—or the total strangers they interact with on the Internet.

They don't have the slightest idea that what is circulated about them today is there forever. It doesn't drop off the Internet just because the item is old. Their posts can haunt them for a lifetime, even erecting barriers to future education, employment, or relationships.

Perhaps they have never been taught the proper boundaries and dangers associated with the Internet. Or maybe they just don't care. Either way, one day they will face the results of the "sowing and reaping" principle. Unfortunately, by then, all they can do is weather the storm they have inadvertently brought into their own lives.

> *Impressions, especially first impressions,*
> *are far more important than you think.*

Growing up, during my teen years and beyond, my mom would "wig-out" if I stepped out of the house without looking as she thought I should. That meant showered, decent clothes (no warm-ups and back then it was those baggy Russell athletic sweats, not the slick, trendy clothes of today), hair in place and make-up on. She would say to me, "If you can, why wouldn't you always look your best?"

At times I would rebel by not washing my hair (pony tail), not putting on make-up, and wearing warm-ups. Now that I am moving from the "Front 9" to the "Back 9," I fully understand her emphasis on these. I'm thankful she stressed the importance of always "putting your best foot forward!" She didn't just highlight looks, she focused on being your best "self!"

Mom totally understood and quoted more than once:

*"You never get a second chance
to make a first impression!"*

In preparing for the Miss America pageant, my training team shined a spotlight on the importance of this principle. They zeroed in on the fact that the first time the judges would lay their eyes on me would be in a photograph. Then they'd proceed to look over my resume. Finally, they would meet me in person during the interview session. Actually, all three of these contributed to my "first impression."

Whoever came up with the phrase, "A picture is worth a thousand words," certainly knew what they were talking about. Whether we care to admit it or not, a photo "speaks" and has much to say. It even allows us to make an instant judgment—whether true or false. This is especially valid if it is a snapshot where we don't have the context.

You've probably seen "mug shots" of people who have been arrested for breaking the law. They look pretty rough. But when we see that same individual standing in a courtroom, there is often a drastic difference in their personal appearance—sometimes a complete makeover. It is because they've been *groomed* to make a good first impression on the judge and jury. Attorneys understand and see the advantage of "putting your best foot forward." It is lived out thousands of times every day in the court system. Lawyers are well aware of human behavior and the influence of "first impressions!"

Remember, whether good or bad, your initial imprint is sometimes the only opportunity you have to impress.

A GENTLE ANSWER

Recently, I watched a young waitress handle an unhappy customer whose order was wrong and late to the table. The server was kind, soft spoken and apologetic. I overheard her say, "What can I do to make this up to you?"

Even though the customer gave a very sarcastic remark, she responded with continued politeness and uncommon self-control. I was so amazed with her poise that when the agitated person left, I told her how impressed I was with how she handled the situation, which was clearly not her fault.

I was pleasantly surprised at her response. "Oh, I have learned to apply Scripture to these situations, such as Proverbs 15:1, 'A gentle answer turns away wrath and a harsh word stirs up anger.'"

My initial impression of that young waitress was stamped and sealed on me. She was a girl with self-control and wisdom, someone who valued her job and didn't mind taking responsibility. Most important, she did it all with a tender heart.

I remember well a day our oldest son, Brewer, and his good friend were talking with a very beautiful young woman who was visiting in our home. In looks, she was flawless. So after she left the scene, I couldn't wait to ask what they thought of her. I was certain they would be enamored. But I was shocked to learn that they were completely turned off!

Since I wasn't involved in their conversation, I wanted to know why they felt this way. They proceeded to tell me that all they heard about were her accomplishments, her current *gig*, and on and on and on—a complete lovefest. They said her "all about me" conversation was a real downer. Sadly, this young woman epitomizes today's "me" generation.

If you had to give yourself a grade of how the cashier at a restaurant, the clerk at an airport check-in, or the receptionist at your doctor's office evaluates you upon first impression, would you receive an "A," a "C," or an "F"?

Personally, I have come to understand more and more how important it is that I radiate the "Jesus" in me—and to do that, I have to spend time with Him in the first part of my day. Otherwise, it is easy to let "self" become my first impression.

TOO MUCH ON OUR PLATES

The subject of *self* brings us to the next major mistake millions make—over-extending themselves.

When our kids were much younger we were out one night eating at our favorite pizza joint.

Collins looked at me in amazement when I quietly turned to her and said, "You do not have to eat everything on your plate."

The boys were too busy chowing down to see the look on her face. In our competitive family, Collins followed the lead of her brothers in just about everything, from golf to eating.

After we returned home that evening, I gently tried to explain how much I loved her wanting to be like her brothers in golf, but she didn't have to mimic them when it came to eating. Trying to be a good teacher, I pointed out that boys had more lean muscle tissue than girls and normally required more food intake. I also mentioned that she was probably not going to be any taller than me, and that paying attention to the little things—perhaps eating just a couple pieces of pizza instead of indulging in five or six—would help her maintain a healthy weight.

LEARNING TO SAY "NO"

Oh, how I loved macaroni and cheese when I was young. I always piled more than necessary on my plate, and before it was gone, I would reach for more.

A childhood tradition was to have lunch at my grand-mother's house every Thursday. One particular day, as I reached for another helping of delicious mac and cheese, my mom said, "Sherry, you already have some on your plate."

I turned and exclaimed, "But I don't want to run out!"

This mimics life. We often put too much on our plate for many reasons, including the fear of saying "no" or attempting to keep up with the Joneses. Whatever the reason, we find ourselves swamped.

I remember a couple in our church, Phillip and Mary Lou, who taught Sunday School for young married adults. As a young mother eager to "do it all," they made a statement that has stuck with me to this day: "Learn to say 'no' with a smile."

My husband and I were raising two young boys and I wanted to serve in the church, be involved in a weekly Bible study, teach, exercise, etc. I found myself saying "yes" to everything and was soon feeling overwhelmed. This couple counseled me on how to seek what God would have me do, not just because the invitations came my way. In those days I was still a "people pleaser," but I learned to filter the requests for my time by taking the matter to the Lord. I guarded my heart (Proverbs 4:23), which resulted in protecting what I did with my hours and days.

In the years since then, there have been several occasions when I ignored that advice and the wheels fell off my wagon. But I recognized the problem, remembered the wise counsel, and got myself back on track.

We certainly don't want to emulate the Pharisees written about in the New Testament. They were so focused on man that they missed out on God's plan for them.

Peter the Apostle said it best: "We ought to obey God rather than men" (Acts 5:29).

Today, I keep enough on my plate to embrace life to the fullest and maximize my gifts and abilities—but not so much that my efforts would be spread too thin. Allow me to quote John Wooden once more. He said, "If you don't have time to do it right, when will you have time to do it over?"

I also like what Rick Warren calls your S.H.A.P.E. — Spiritual gifts, Heart/passion, Abilities, Personality, Experiences.

Today, I still teach our kids (now young adults) to examine their "plate of life," and that a healthy serving might mean less! I believe the Lord calls different folks to different strokes. Just as in golf, you can hit the same shot different ways and achieve the same great outcome.

Please let me encourage you to take a close look at you plate of life. Ask yourself:

- Is there too much? Not enough?
- Are there too many starches (bad stuff)?
- Do I need more vegetables (good stuff)?
- Or do I need meat, something a little harder to chew on (provide sustained nourishment)?

It's only natural to be concerned that we will not do enough, or that we won't do the right things. When the sisters, Mary and Martha were entertaining Jesus in their home, the Lord reminded Martha, who was rushing around the kitchen preparing food, of what was most important: "Martha, Martha...you are worried and upset about many things, but few things are needed—or indeed only one. Mary has chosen what is better [to be at the Lord's side], and it will not be taken away from her" (Luke 10:41-42 NIV).

Why make the mistake of experiencing burnout by having too much on your plate?

*Realize that doing the best with less is
far better than doing less with more!*

TAMING THE MONSTER!

Another major mistake has a color attached to it. We

jokingly refer to it as "the green-eyed monster" because of the phrase "green with envy."

I find it hard to believe a person who says they have never dealt with jealousy. This is an emotion deeply embedded in the human psyche. As Paul the Apostle wrote long ago, "For since there is jealousy and quarreling among you, are you not worldly? Are you not acting like mere humans?" (1 Corinthian 3:3 NIV). Even as believers, we still deal with the lure of the "flesh."

Jealousy is a temptation and a character trait we need to pay special attention to—rather than thinking we have this area mastered. Envy is sneaky, and often camouflages and masks other issues. This is why it's so difficult to get beneath the surface or "peel the onion" in our own lives and ultimately rid ourselves of the monster.

Proverbs 14:30 tells us that "envy is rottenness to the bones." And we are advised that "if you have bitter envy and self-seeking in your hearts, do not boast and lie against the truth" (James 3:14).

In my observations, jealousy is most often seen in women, especially young and maturing girls! I am so thankful to have a daughter, who I now call a "best friend," even though I often wear my "mother hat."

With that being said, Collins and I have had long discussions on the topic of jealousy: (a) being jealous and (b) being the victim of jealousy.

Envy is exposed when we are on the receiving end. It's

then we realize, "Wrath is cruel and anger is a torrent, but who is able to stand before jealousy?" (Proverbs 27:4). In other words, envy trumps almost everything.

If you have ever been a target, you know how hurtful this can be. But it should cause you to ask yourself, "If this feels so awful, is there a possibility that I have been jealous and inflicted this pain on someone else?" Maybe you were so "blind" to your envy that you didn't even realize the anguish you were causing.

As a senior in high school, I can remember coming home from winning South Carolina's Junior Miss. The next morning, hanging in a tree outside my window was a dummy of me on fire!

Jealousy?

I also vividly remember my sister driving a new car to high school only to come out after class to find that someone had put a live chicken in her car for the day. It practically destroyed the inside of the vehicle.

Jealousy? I think so.

I have previously mentioned social media, but it is a place where envy is constantly coming to the forefront. For example, can you imagine the feelings of a young girl who goes on Facebook Saturday morning and finds out she was excluded from a class pajama party the night before? The sting of rejection can create a bonfire of hurt feelings and the embers can smoulder indefinitely.

*From my vantage point, if you sincerely ask
the Lord to show you a weakness, or even a "sin"
that is lurking in your life, He will.*

Allow Him to expose any "slimy green monster" that may be lingering in the hidden crevices of your life.

The best antidote to jealousy is an "inward focus." I'm not talking about self-centeredness, but asking God to reveal your heart, to show you your uniqueness and talents. Also ask for grace to be "sincerely happy" for a friend who has achieved more success than you. The Lord desires for us to be compassionate and generous in our love for others; when we are, He will pour out His unmerited favor on us.

In competitive golf, I have purposed and prayed to be truly grateful when others succeed, especially ahead of my kids. God has been faithful to move my spirit in that direction, but this didn't just come naturally. I had to ask for it. Even then I had to guard my heart with Scripture and fight the temptation to let Satan whisper in my ear the alternative.

I know only too well that when you seek to do the right thing, the enemy will try every trick in his arsenal to defeat you and gain back lost ground. Being genuinely happy for someone else goes against our nature—and the devil wants to keep it that way.

Like Job, if the Lord ceased blessing my life, I should still be grateful and filled with thankfulness for all He has done.

As Paul wrote, "Not that I speak in regard to need, for I

have learned that whatever state I am, to be content" (Philippians 4:11).

This peace comes with purposed intention, meaning you must hunger for and seek it out.

Let me encourage you to go on a hunting trip to finally capture the "green-eyed monster." Most likely, you won't have to travel far!

HOW'S THAT WORKING FOR YOU?

Giving in to jealousy, is just one of the hooks or slices that can take you off course.

Looking back on your journey, you may say, "Sherry, if I made a list of all the bloopers and blunders I've peppered through my life, I'd run out of ink and paper."

We all make mistakes, but in an effort to change directions, I've had to stop every once in a while and ask myself, "How's that working out for you?" Then I reflect on the old adage: "If you do what you have always done, you get what you have always gotten."

I used that question and this statement on our kids so long that, when necessary, they turn them around and use them on me!

You are never too young or too old to want to escape repeating the same old mistakes. It's a cop out to think otherwise, and nothing but an excuse to become obstinate, lazy, and not willing to step out and do something different.

Of course, old habits die hard and are difficult to break, but with God's help—and by His design—we can all make changes.

Where does this "new you" start? Since all actions are preceded by thoughts, it begins in the mind and heart. It is vital to pay attention to this principle from the Word: "Do not be conformed to this world, but be transformed by the renewing of your mind, that you may prove what is that good and acceptable and perfect will of God" (Romans 12:2).

TIME FOR A NEW ROUTINE

If you want freedom from the ruts of your past mistakes, you need a game plan. In other words, you have to discard some of your old patterns and adopt new, productive ones.

Most great golfers establish a pre-shot routine. It's a very effective method of improving one's focus on the task at hand, which is to hit the next shot. For example, in driving the ball or in putting, our son Thomas has a drill he repeats every time he gets ready to hit the ball. On the drive, he steps on the tee box, tees the ball up, stands behind it, and picks his target (where he is aiming). He then steps back and takes two practice swings, then he addresses the ball and hits it. This never varies.

The routine is widely accepted by most celebrated golfers as a way to feel comfortable and at ease. It helps bring you into extreme focus.

In my own life, to make sincere changes and find new directions (I call them '180s'), I have to decide to decide. Then I have to follow through with actions—which are simple, but take tremendous discipline to carry out.

The following is my pre-day schedule that I have established to have the most effective quiet time with God.

At night I set my alarm for 5:30 A.M. I picked a place in our house for my "alone" time that is away from everyone. I bought an iPod and play soft Christian music in the background. I have a vitamin and energy drink, my Bible, my journal, pen, and laptop (I use my laptop to look up passages or commentaries on Scripture for deeper learning and understanding).

In addition, I always have a good book on hand that I am currently reading, usually something written by an inspiring Christian author or a biography.

> *As I have committed to this regimen,*
> *and have followed it faithfully for the past*
> *several years, it has enabled me to make*
> *some rather significant changes.*

When I first started, I was amazed at how the music invited my heart, not only to worship, but it warmed the room where I was sitting. When you awaken in the morning and everything is cloaked in quietness and darkness, turning on a light and hearing some soft music transforms the environment. It affects my mood, soothes my spirit, and gives me the atmosphere of praise needed to prepare my heart to receive all that God has for me.

As this routine was established, it became a place where I was excited to spend time, to the point that sometimes I would wake up at 4:00 or 4:30 A.M. and start early because I loved the result of the obedience—and the intimacy of God's presence I received in that hour. I wanted more.

A MAJOR TURN-AROUND

Most psychologists will tell you that a pre-shot routine can also be a place of comfort for a golfer. If they are not having a good day on the links, it provides security and satisfaction.

I have found this to be exactly the case for me in my daily devotional time. If I am tired, or facing a stressful situation, it is a welcoming place of peace, security, and tranquility. It becomes a time where God's Word speaks to me personally. It is my place of refuge.

I have gleaned these benefits through the discipline of creating a daily meeting time with God. He is always there and ready. I just have to show up and be obedient.

The reason I want to share this with you is because before beginning this new schedule, my time with the Lord had been whatever minutes I could squeeze in. I didn't have a specific time to meet with God, nor a particular place. I discovered I needed a set routine that included meeting with my heavenly

Father before my day begins.

I would never dream of going out of the house without combing my hair and brushing my teeth, so why in the world would I face my day without first meeting with my Creator and the Author of my life?

As in a golfer's pre-shot pattern, my pre-day routine of meeting with the Lord has become key to major successes in my life. It has allowed the renewing of my mind and has revealed His will for me. In fact, it is where He birthed the *Back Nine Ministries.*

God had a plan for the second half of my life, and I shudder to think what I would have missed if I had not taken the steps to make a change.

In one of Michael Jackson's all time most popular songs, "Man in the Mirror," he wrote and sang, "I'm starting with the man in the mirror. I'm asking him to change his ways, and no message could have been any clearer, If you wanna make the world a better place—take a look at yourself, and then make a change."

Your transformation begins with a thought (decision) followed by action, and a relationship with your Maker.

It's time to say farewell to the mistakes of your past. You can start again today!

NOTES FOR YOUR SCORECARD

- You can master your tongue through silence, forgiveness, prayer, confronting properly, letting go, and realizing everything starts with the heart.
- Two wrongs never make a right.
- Pay close attention to "first impressions" and how others see you.
- Avoid over-extending yourself by learning to say "No."
- Overcome envy by asking the Lord to give you a genuine love for others.
- Establish a game plan to discard negative patterns and adopt new, productive ones.
- Make time with the Lord an essential part of your daily "pre shot" routine.

TEE #6
ADVERSITY

*N*o one escapes adversity. It doesn't acknowledge skin color, bank accounts, accomplishments, who "your daddy is," or play favorites.

Trouble and hardship have no timetable and know no calendar. They can arrive dressed pretty and deceiving, or may appear ugly and grow even uglier! But one thing is for sure; at one time or another they will knock on everyone's door. Adversity is like the hide-and-seek game we played as kids: "Ready or not, here I come."

Thankfully, nothing takes God by surprise. In fact, trials are one of God's paths for our development. We are told, "Consider it pure joy, my brothers and sisters, whenever you face trials of many kinds, because you know that the testing of your faith produces perseverance. Let perseverance finish its work so that you may be mature and complete not lacking anything" (James 1:2-4 NIV).

Consider means to embrace, which should cause us to ask some pertinent questions:

- Was it my decision that caused this problem?
- If so, what can I do differently next time?
- What was my sin, and do I need to repent?
- What can I learn from this?
- How can I look to God and His Word to grow my faith?

In the above verse we are told the purpose of a trial is to test our faith, trust, and belief. Plus it serves to give us spiritual maturity and helps us become "whole." If handled properly, adversity can lead us to new, purpose-filled places.

Facing the Unexpected

At the age of 35, devastation knocked on the door of our home. Adversity arrived in the form of a disease that attacked our son, Thomas, who was five years old at the time.

He was diagnosed with Type 1 diabetes. So innocent, so small, and still a thumb-sucker, he now faced a life with a disease for which there was no cure. His future would be dependent on insulin and needles (millions of sticks) for the rest of his life.

For a mother, there are not enough words to adequately describe the pain of the hurricane that ripped through our lives. It was unexpected, foreign to us, scary, heart-breaking, and all-consuming. This was way bigger than anything I personally felt the ability to handle and master.

It was truly a tight-rope walk, a test of trust and faith in God. To survive, I began leaning more heavily on God for comfort. I also had to depend on others placed in my life during this season for information and help. It was a challenge to learn and grasp the management of this illness. I knew I would eventually have to transfer this knowledge to Thomas as he grew older.

After seven days in the hospital, we returned home hoping for normalcy, but we quickly learned we were living a "new normal."

I found myself praying hourly. I wasn't exactly thrilled to travel this path, but constant prayer brought about an intimacy with God that I had never before experienced. His peace would wash over me like a warm blanket, calming my fears of the unknown and the inadequacy I felt.

WHAT SHOULD I DO?

Without question, adversity gives you eyes to see the Lord more clearly.

When you are taken to a place where things are completely out of your control, it causes you to look up in total helplessness to see the mighty hand of an all-powerful God.

Through difficulties, you certainly learn who your friends are. In this particular trial, some of the most comforting gestures came from those who asked, "What can I do to help you?"—and did it! The ones who came alongside us to assist in providing Thomas with a healthy, safe environment in which to thrive. They gave me much-needed breaks and peace of mind to know he was in the loving hands of people who genuinely cared. These individuals, many years later, still write notes of prayer and encouragement to Thomas.

Trials and difficulties expose both our weaknesses and our need for God. They are the fires of life the Lord uses to refine who we are and reveal who He is. When faced with them, it is important to:

1. Turn to God, not away from Him

Trying to solve every problem with your own powers of reasoning is not only futile, but an act of pride. And you know what comes after pride—a fall. So instead of chasing your own shadow, make a U-turn and head in the direction of the One who has the ultimate answer.

2. Embrace it

Rejecting, or refusing to acknowledge a misfortune, may prolong what you need to learn. One lesson I personally received through this experience with our son was *compassion.*

Until this condition entered our home, I just *thought* I was a compassionate person. Oddly enough, but certainly one of God's lessons for me, was the fact that two years before Thomas was diagnosed with the disease, our next door neighbor's 12-year-old son was told he suffered with Type 1 diabetes.

Yes, I was concerned and prayed for the family, but had no real concept of their pain and the life-altering upheaval diabetes brought to their family until we were flung into the same situation. After leaving the hospital where Thomas was diagnosed, one of the very first things on my to-do list was to head straight over to our neighbor's house and apologize for my lack of sensitivity and my truly apathetic response.

It completely changed my attitude toward the pain of others, even if I have not walked in their shoes. I now make it a point to try and understand and empathize with what someone else is going through, and to be a godly friend.

3. Pray and ask others to join you, even if you aren't sure what words to say

There are times when "we do not know what we should pray for as we ought, but the Spirit Himself makes intercession for us with groanings which cannot be uttered" (Romans 8:26).

When you fall to your knees and spend time in prayer, it brings amazing peace and strength.

Our children ask me to pray for them often, and it is my joy to do so. But I let them know that there is nothing more powerful on the planet than to personally, fervently talk with the Lord about something persistently and see Him move on their behalf.

Sometimes we don't receive the answers we are looking for, yet down the road we can usually see the advantages of God's wisdom in either delaying, or saying "No."

I recently read the news story about a young teen who's father did not allow him to go to the beach with friends on a particular Saturday; he made him stay home and study. On the way back from the shore, five of his close friends were killed in a tragic car accident. Before that horrible news, I'm sure the teen wasn't happy with his dad's decision, but it inevitably saved his life!

I have no idea of the "whys" or the timing of those deaths, yet I know that sometimes the answers we don't want to hear are for our greater good.

4. Read God's Word

Search the Scriptures to find the comfort, direction, and purpose He provides for those who love Him. The psalmist wrote, "Many are the afflictions of the righteous, but the Lord delivers him out of them all" (Psalm 34:19).

5. *Journal*

Narrative therapy can help you expose your feelings. A written account also serves as a way to help others with what they are going through. When you journal, especially during adversity, it allows you a very safe place to vent, I have specifically found that writing about my pain, anger, and frustration, allows me to release my steam and purge these harmful feelings. Later, when I go back and read my thoughts, I realize it was an escape for me. This has also helped me from being tempted to share with someone who perhaps I shouldn't.

At times, the most difficult thing for anyone to see is themselves. Since we are with ourselves 24 hours a day, all we know is what we have experienced. Yet others see us in a different light.

Part of our basic instinct is to like who we are, hopefully because we are created in God's image. But we walk a fine line with pride, liking ourselves so much that we become blind to personal traits that need altering.

IT HITS HOME

Adversity takes on many forms. It even showed up in our home under the guise of bullying.

I remember walking out of an annual Christmas party when my cell phone rang. It was our son, Thomas, then a senior in high school. Even before talking, I had an uncanny feeling that he was calling with an emergency.

As I answered, I braced myself and could hear all kinds of noise in the background. Thomas, who is a cool-headed kid, was audibly upset and wanted us to hurry home immediately. It was about our daughter, Collins.

She was a sophomore at the time and had been experiencing bullying behavior in school. That evening, in a recreational league basketball game, she had been purposely hit in the head with a basketball. The girl who did this was given a technical foul and was thrown out of the game.

Based on the past bullying, Thomas was alarmed that it had escalated and become physical. He was the strong, supportive brother, but I don't think he trusted himself; he was afraid of losing control.

My husband and I were over two hours away, and on the drive back I couldn't help but think of being bullied myself. I mentioned earlier that after winning South Carolina's Junior Miss contest, someone hung an effigy of me on a tree outside my window and set it on fire.

When we arrived home, Collins told us the whole story.

After she was hit, and just before the girl was ejected from the game, the guilty party said, "I did this for my friend." It's amazing how bullies can often get others to do their dirty work. The good news is that the girl who hit Collins later apologized and they became friends.

UNPLANNED-FOR ROCKS

Out of the blue, we can suddenly be blindsided by "unplanned-for" rocks.

Being a road builder, my father would often load up the family on the weekend and drive around, surveying the progress being made on the new roads he was constructing.

I have vivid memories of freshly-graded soil and piles of brush and trees burning as they would clear land to make way for a new highway. It was always a stressful time for my dad when he hit "unexpected rock," meaning there were boulders undetected through soil tests during the bidding process. When he initially calculated and submitted a bid to win the job, he didn't factor in the cost of having to dynamite and remove these rocks.

In order to handle such surprises, and the expense connected with them, he would work longer hours and on Saturdays to meet deadlines and offset the unplanned cost.

I witnessed first hand my dad, a man of strong faith, diligently adjusting to the situation at hand and having the fortitude to handle the unexpected.

These images taught me early on that everyone gets hit by unexpected "rocks," but my dad showed me how to handle them.

We have to look at the bigger picture, not panic, and realize that detours and diversions are part of life.

SHARING AN ADVERSITY

Recently I met a brand new friend, Jan, from the neighboring state of North Carolina. She is a friend of a friend, who thought Jan and I should meet at a Starbucks.

I quickly learned we had many things in common—our mutual friend, our faith, and the fact that all three of us shared major life-changing adversities.

It was a three-hour unexpected conversation hearing about her life, but especially her "unplanned rock"—the sudden death of her 27-year-old son, James. She told how she awoke one morning with a very-much-alive son and went to bed the same night with a son who was dead.

James had been serving on the mission field and was in Nairobi, Kenya, when she lost him. He died of pneumonia. I could only imagine the shock and pain she endured.

We talked about our friend, Sheryl, who was still in the midst of deep grief from the loss of her husband, Bob. As we shared tears, smiles and life in general, it was a tremendous solace to see how the "Rock of Ages" had faithfully sustained all three of us.

The psalmist gives us this uplifting reminder: "The Lord is my rock and my fortress and my deliverer; my God, my strength, in whom I will trust; my shield and the horn of my salvation, my stronghold" (Psalms 18:2).

For Jan's family their loss was tremendous. I will never forget the scripture she quoted to me: "Very truly I tell you, unless a kernel of wheat falls to the ground and dies, it remains only a single seed. But if it dies, it produces many seeds" (John 12:24 NIV).

Through their pain and loss of James, the foundation she and her husband, Frank, began (www.withopeneyes.net) has grown exponentially.

I love how God used Jan to further grow my faith in the area of applying Scripture and actions to the "rocks" life throws our way. At one time or another, we all become targets—sometimes being hit by multiple rocks at once.

How blessed we are to know where to turn
for divine strength, support, and guidance.

"MOM, WHY?"

Rocks and bad news will cause us to ask this probing question: "Why?"

When devastating tornadoes ripped through Oklahoma, I received a letter on my Facebook inbox from a concerned young mother who was struggling to give an appropriate answer to her young child's questions about what they had been seeing on the news.

The little girl asked. "Mom, why did God let that awful thing happen?"

I pondered for a week before answering. Not knowing her

child personally, I wanted to pray and think carefully what the Lord would have me to say.

A storm can produce extreme destruction and heartache, and I do believe God has power over the weather. But if we go back to Genesis, Adam and Eve (man) brought sin, chaos, and death into the world from the pride of wanting to be like the Creator.

This side of heaven we can never fully comprehend all the do's and don'ts of why God does what He does or what He allows. We can know, however, that bad things happen to good people—not just storms, but disease, accidents, murder, starvation, etc. However, all the *ugly* started with the first sin in the garden of Eden. This changed God's perfect plan for earth and the human race.

The Bible speaks clearly about storms and nature, that God pours down rain on both the righteous and unrighteous. The underlying message is that we must turn to the Lord in times of trouble and seek Him.

Death is an inevitable part of life. We aren't designed to choose the way our journey will end, but one thing is for certain, we will all meet our Maker one day.

Teaching our children (or anyone for that matter) about adversity and heartache is never easy, especially if someone is experiencing a life storm. But comfort and understanding is ours when we know God and the heart He has for all of His creation.

Some individuals experience pain as a result of their own

actions, but other devastation is a consequence of the fall of man in the garden. I thank God for His redemption that was completed when He sent His Son to die and rise again. Through His resurrection we can accept the offer to overcome eternal death through salvation.

WOUNDED—DEEPLY WOUNDED

From talking with thousands of people over the years, I've come to the conclusion that at some point in life, every person is wounded—deeply wounded. I am not referring to a biting word, action, or inaction by an individual, but something that has caused deep, pulsating pain!

In the past few days I have talked with five men and women who have gone through what I am talking about:

1. Friends (a couple) who are hurt over their separation/divorce, but they lack people, especially Christians, to reach out to them.
2. A girl in college whose dad abandoned her as a young child. The father remarried and has more kids, but she has been kicked to the curb by him. Her mother lives in bitterness and anger, and the young woman feels lost and alone.
3. A man coming into adulthood has chosen Jesus and is endeavoring to live the Christian life, but has been abandoned by his "former friends."

4. A woman who invested much of her life in something that has been unfairly taken away from her. She is now dealing with the insensitivity of people who she thought loved and supported her.

5. One of my former college friends who arrived at work and found her co-worker dead—hanging by a rope in her office.

Life can be hard, cruel, and painful. If you live long enough you will be hit by arrows you didn't see coming. Whether we are wounded directly or indirectly, innocently or on purpose, the resulting torment can be the same.

Then comes the question: what do we do when we find ourselves gushing emotional blood?

I can only speak from personal experience. I am always learning, and may be imperfect in my execution at times, but the Lord has taught me a few things on this topic in the five-plus decades I've been on this planet.

Earlier, we discussed specific things to do if you have been wounded, but let me offer these additional suggestions:

First: Run to God!

This advice may sound simplistic, but when you are hurting, don't curl up in a fetal position and wallow in a pity-party. Instead, lace up your spiritual track shoes and head in the direction of your heavenly Father as fast as you can!

Even if you haven't talked or prayed in weeks, years, or

ever, run to Him. You don't have to recite eloquent prayers, just a sincere heart to know Him, experience Him, and pour out your innermost feelings. He will show up and begin the healing process. We have this promise: "A bruised reed he will not break, and a smoldering wick he will not snuff out, till he has brought justice through victory" (Matthew 12:20 and Isaiah 53:5 NIV).

And we are told that "by his [Jesus'] wounds we are healed" (Isaiah 53:5 NIV).

Second: Consider Christian counseling

A safe place to voice your suffering is in the office of a professional, licensed counselor who is a Christian. Such a person can help direct and promote a path of healing. Be willing to be honest and cast off pride (not caring about what he or she may think), seeking to give the entire, truthful picture, exposing and admitting your own mistakes.

Honesty is necessary to get to the root of the wound. Then be willing to take appropriate steps to recover.

> *Realize that fear is never from God, but from your enemy, so cast it aside.*

Please don't allow anxiety to stop you from seeking relief; it may be just the catalyst needed to motivate you to find help.

Third: Attend church regularly

Even if you go by yourself, there's nothing like being brave enough to find your place in the house of God. Come with an attitude of worship and expect to feel His presence—not just to socialize and be around other people.

The joy you will receive from a desire to look for the Lord is beyond description. He makes this vow: "You will seek Me and find Me, when you search for Me with all your heart (Jeremiah 29:13). God always keeps His Word; He does not lie.

Fourth: Read the right books

There are hundreds, even thousands of wonderful books available to you. Let me recommend that you browse the shelves of a Christian bookstore (or the Christian section of a store such as Barnes & Noble). You'll find topics that target the very problem you are dealing with. On the Internet, Google Charles Stanley, Andy Stanley, Joyce Meyer, Perry Noble, or a local church. Today there are countless sermons online that will address your needs. Watch and listen to them carefully and prayerfully—then put what is recommended into practice.

YOU MAY HAVE THE ANSWER

We have been dealing with our own hurts, but let's look at the other half of the equation. How do you help a friend or loved one who is going through a tough time in life?

If I had not experienced pain and hardship, I would not be able to relate well to others who are in a similar situation. There is a biblical foundation for this. We are told, "Endure hardship as discipline; God is treating you as his children. For what children are not disciplined by their father?...No discipline seems pleasant at the time, but painful. Later on, however, it produces a harvest of righteousness and peace for those who have been trained by it. Therefore, strengthen your feeble arms and weak knees? 'Make level paths for your feet,' so that the lame may not be disabled, but rather healed" (Hebrews 12:7,11-14 NIV).

We learn how to help a friend in need through our own wounds that have been healed by the Lord.

Let me recommend these five steps for you to take when someone is despondent:

Step #1: Pray, pray, and pray!

It's our natural tendency to rush in and give personal advice to a friend who is facing adversity. There is a time and a place for this, but the first gift you should give them is to take their situation to the Lord in prayer. Not only will God hear, but if you listen He will give you the right words to say when the time comes.

Step #2: Talk

When a friend is in pain, they may interpret your silence as an indicator of "not caring." So when that individual unburdens their heart to you, let them know that you will be praying for them. Then get back to the person as soon as possible to share what the Lord is leading you to say.

If you still don't have the right words, reassure them that you love them—and "Because you hurt, I am hurting too."

Hug them, mail them a card, send them an email or a text to their inbox, or buy them a book that addresses their pain.

Doing nothing is not the answer. Please don't remain silent.

Step #3: Invite them to church

The man or woman going through a valley often feels alone, so offer to take them to church next Sunday. Your fellowship is what they will respond to, but the message they will hear may be exactly what is needed for a complete turn-around.

Step #4: Be aware of others who are suffering

Whether we know it or not, every day we come in contact with people who are under tremendous pressure because of a circumstance of which we are not aware. Keep your antenna up! Pick up any signal that there may be hidden pain behind their smile. Just a small conversation beyond, "How's it going?" may open a floodgate that allows that person to unburden their heart.

Even to a stranger, a kind word can be a "cold drink in a desert." You could literally be taking the gun out of their hand that they have been silently holding to their head.

Step #5: It is never too late to reach out

If you have failed in the past to reach out to someone whose heart is crying, today may be the day.

I missed out on knowing that a friend from my past had lost their mother. It had been four years. So I sat down and wrote her a belated sympathy letter. Shortly after, I received a wonderful reply, letting me know that my letter had arrived on the anniversary of her mom's birthday. I had no idea, but it was current, real medicine on a wound that was still fresh for her—even though it had been four years.

> *It is God's place to heal, but it is our*
> *place to love, support, and care.*

Problems? Trials? Obstacles? Adversity? They are all part of living in an imperfect world. However, the good news is that we don't have to cross the river alone. There is a hand of mercy reaching down to help us reach the other side.

With God's help, yours can be a hand of mercy, too.

NOTES FOR YOUR SCORECARD

- Nothing takes the Lord by surprise—not even your adversity.
- When faced with a problem, (1) turn to God, not away from Him, (2) embrace the situation, (3) pray, and ask others to join you, (4) read God's Word, and (5) journal.
- If unexpected rocks appear in your path, accept the fact that detours and diversions are part of life.
- When you are emotionally wounded, (1) run to the Lord quickly, (2) consider Christian counseling, (3) attend church regularly, and (4) read helpful books—especially the Bible.
- If friends face adversity, (1) take their needs to the Lord in prayer, (2) communicate with them; silence usually sends the wrong message, (3) invite them to attend church with you, (4) remain aware of their needs, and (5) realize that it's never too late to reach out.
- With God's help, you can offer a hand of mercy.

TEE #7
CONFIDENCE

*A*s a youngster, someone probably read you the children's classic, *The Little Engine That Could.*

It's the story of a train with a heavy load that needed to be pulled over a high mountain. After larger engines had tried and failed, a small engine, half their size, agreed to make the attempt. It was successful, all the while repeating its motto: "I think I can! I think I can! I think I can!"

Today, millions of men, women, and children need that same assurance. All they see are the craggy mountains ahead, and they don't know how to conquer them. On this tee I want to share six "confidence builders" that will fuel the engine of your life and give you the strength to succeed.

Confidence-Builder #1: Learn from Experience Until You Master Your Subject

I recently met a woman who had read a number of my blogs at www.back9ministries.org. She commented, "It must have been wonderful growing up around the game of golf."

She was surprised when I told her, "I had never stepped

121

my foot on a golf course until after I was married." In fact, I can still remember when and where it happened the first time.

As a newlywed, I went along with my husband, Bill, and one of his college buddies, Fred, to the historic Linville Golf Club. They were entered in a four-ball tournament at this beautiful mountain course in North Carolina.

I was just there to watch. After they teed off, I was going to catch them at the 10th hole right after the turn. For you non-golfers, that means on the "back 9" of 18 holes.

I had a golf cart, so I decided to park in what I thought would be the perfect spot with the best view. Back then my eyesight was 20/20 and I saw Bill in the distance frantically waving his arms. I thought he was motioning for help, and he was! He was helping save me from extreme embarrassment. Little did I know that the place I had parked was on the 11th tee box!

Most people on a course like Linville would be familiar with golf etiquette—especially if you were allowed to have a spectator cart and watch a tournament. I was parked on the box where the group in front of Bill was walking to tee off. I literally thought those markers were like a "designated spot" for a cart and it was first-come, first-served for spectators.

This is why I say, "You don't know what you don't know."

I've come a long way since then. The confidence I have in talking about golf has been accumulated from years of being with our kids as they became totally immersed in mastering the sport. Their knowledge has certainly rubbed off on me.

Confidence-Builder #2: Be Comfortable in Your Own Skin

Relax! Don't be anxious or become a bundle of nerves over things which you have no control. Realize that you are the world's greatest authority on one topic: what has happened to you.

> *No one else can tell your story or*
> *give your opinion as well as you can.*

I've been put on the spot more than once. When it was time for the contestants in the Miss South Carolina pageant to be interviewed, the second question I was asked by a judge was, "Since you are a business major, what do you think of the decision Coca-Cola made to change their recipe for Coke?"

I couldn't believe the seven words that shot out of my mouth. Without missing a beat, I answered, "If it ain't broke, don't fix it!"

Suddenly, every judge sitting at the table started laughing. In my mind, I thought, "Well, I really blew it." So I tried to chuckle with them while explaining my answer. I said to myself, "Sherry, you used the word 'ain't'—they must think you are a country bumpkin."

The rest of the interview went well, including the fact that I could speak somewhat intelligently about Wimbledon. I knew Boris Becker had won, even though I had never played tennis.

After I was presented with the state title, I met with the judges to be critiqued and prepare for the Miss America pageant. I was told that after each interview the judges have a short discussion. If the contestant impresses them, they usually make some comment such as, "Boy, I hope she's got talent and looks fit in a swim suit, because she was great in the interview."

If you can't speak intelligently, clearly communicate your views, and charm the judges, regardless of whether they agree with your convictions or not, you don't stand a chance. I've come to the conclusion that you can't win with *only* the interview, but you can lose it all if you bomb it.

The morning after I was crowned, Donna Axum (a former Miss America) told me that my answer about Coke, "If it ain't broke, don't fix it," was so refreshing that it won the interview for me.

So what I thought I had done wrong, was the one thing I did right!

Since that time, in countless situations, instead of worrying over what I might say, I decided to just be myself.

Confidence-Builder #3: Welcome Competition

Why are the television ratings so high for the Super Bowl or a presidential election? It's because there is a contest involved and we can't wait to see who wins—and who loses.

I've spent most of my adult life watching our kids compete and I believe there's not a person alive who doesn't want to experience the thrill of victory. I still get excited every time my Clemson Tigers win a football game!

A few summers ago, I was caddying for our middle son, Thomas, in a huge state amateur event. He had never won a tournament at this level before.

At the end of 15 holes, he was tied for the lead with his playing partner, who had won previous amateur events. Thomas birdied number 16 and his partner had a bogey, giving him a two-shot lead. Then they both pared number 17.

My eyes were riveted with anticipation as I stood near the 18th tee. I realized that Thomas' first big win was within reach if he could just hang on.

It was a surreal moment when he holed the winning putt and our family, friends, and the media rushed to congratulate him.

Winning is special, and I was humbled, thankful, tearful, and speechless—all at the same time.

Yet, victory is fleeting. You begin to wonder when the next win is coming, and the cycle starts all over again. While we welcome competition, the real battle is fought within ourselves.

What I have learned over the years is that victory is exhilarating and wonderful, but self-assurance is developed by staying on the front lines. Every loss is a stepping stone. Every near-win gives you a glimpse of what is possible.

*It is the constant trying that builds
faith and belief which eventually lets you
reach the top of the mountain.*

Confidence Builder #4:
Develop Personal Initiative

It seems that all my life I have been immersed in a contest of one kind or another—whether going for a world clogging championship, a "Miss" something title, or encouraging our kids in golf.

Early on, I realized that my "personal initiative" was the only factor which I controlled. Others had their own agendas; but I gave up worrying over their skills or experience. There were three reasons I felt this way.

- First, I knew that because of prayer and living a surrendered life to Christ, He was guiding my path.
- Second, because I knew God was leading, I felt that no matter the outcome, I was confident that this was what I was supposed to be doing.

- Third, I kept my "eyes and focus" on my talents, abilities, and initiative.
- Fourth, with God's help, I realized that I could only control what I did, not the actions of anyone else.

In pageants, I was so zoned in on "personal initiative" that to this day I couldn't tell you what the other contestants sang or to what music they danced.

When we stop agonizing about "beating" someone who may be a "frontrunner" in a contest, it allows us to unclutter our minds and be directed internally by what the Lord speaks in our hearts. This keeps our eyes on our God-given abilities and gives us the freedom to accomplish our purpose.

If we aren't careful, we can fall into the "comparison trap," trying to "one up" another contestant. This can lead to making us feel as if we are second class, creating a lack of initiative and originality.

The professionals who have worked with our children in golf have pounded into them the importance of focusing on the *process* of what they are working to achieve. They learned to take their eyes off everything and everyone and concentrate on what they were doing.

I remind our children, "You are on a journey with a purpose in which God created you to fulfill." Jesus outlined the priorities that lead to success: "But seek first the kingdom of God and His righteousness, and all these things shall be added to you" (Matthew 6:33).

Confidence-Builder #5:
Don't Listen to Your Doubts

For whatever reason, I often hear negative voices whispering in my ear on Sundays. I've heard them at other times, but primarily on God's Day.

In recent years, I have come to recognize this as the voice of the enemy. In case you aren't aware, we have an evil foe whose name is Satan—and he is very real. This is why we are warned, "Be sober, be vigilant; because your adversary the devil walks about like a roaring lion, seeking whom he may devour" (1 Peter 5:8).

Most of the time, the way the enemy tries to devour me is by whispering lies of discouragement and instilling doubts. His goal is to destroy our dreams and crush our confidence.

I remember the day he lied to me as I walked into church: "You are not worthy or 'holy' enough to launch a ministry." Then he said, "Look at the people around you. They are in church much more than you because you're always off to another golf tournament. How will anyone take you seriously?"

Through wise counsel and spending time in God's Word, I have grown by leaps and bounds in my walk with the Lord—and have become better equipped to distinguish the clear voice of God from the whisper of the enemy.

Satan is tricky, "a wolf in sheep's clothing," and he can easily fool us. It helps me to breathe a quick prayer like this one: "God I know You love me and desire the best for me. I ask You in the name of Jesus to bind the enemy and make him flee. You are a God of hope, not of discouragement. Please allow me to hear Your voice louder and to obey fully."

The murmurings from the enemy quickly fade and disappear. This simple prayer brings much needed peace and redirects my focus to God and away from fear, doubt, or "people pleasing." Psalm 143:1 emphasizes this: "Lord hear my prayer, listen to my cry for mercy; in your faithfulness and righteousness come to my relief."

Instead of turning toward your doubts, turn your ear toward heaven. You will hear a still small voice that will fill you with purpose and power.

"In quietness and confidence shall be your strength" (Isaiah 30:15).

Confidence-Builder #6:
Surrender to the Ultimate Source of Confidence

"Surrender" is not a word anyone wants to hear. It implies losing or giving up. No one wants to be a loser!

In our culture, being on top of your game gets you the most admiration, publicity, and, usually, money. Winners can hardly wait to look into the television camera and excitedly exclaim, "I'm going to Disney World!"

In God's economy, however confidence comes as the result of a totally different set of rules. Paul the Apostle states it this way: " I urge you, brothers and sisters, in view of God's mercy, to offer your bodies as a living sacrifice [surrender], holy and pleasing to God—this is your true and proper worship. Do not conform to the pattern of this world, but be transformed by the renewing of your mind. Then you will be able to test and approve what God's will is—his good, pleasing and perfect will" (Romans 12:1-2 NIV).

The Lord knows how easy it is for us to get caught up in what is temporal—like winning. This is why we are told to break away from "the pattern of this world."

True victory comes from a life totally yielded to our Creator. As Wiliam Booth, founder of the Salvation Army, said, "The greatness of man's power is in the measure of his surrender."

Trust is key. It's easy to give up control to someone in whom you have faith and confidence.

One of my favorite Bible stories describes how Peter had been fishing all night on the Sea of Galilee and hadn't even caught a minnow. Then Jesus told him, to go back and "Launch out into the deep and let down your nets for a catch" (Luke 5:4).

When Peter listened, surrendered, and trusted, he and his friends caught so many fish that their nets were ripping under the weight—and when they tried to pull the nets into the boat, it almost sank!

What a thrill to know that we can place our trust in One

who has "all-knowing vision."

Author and pastor Rick Warren put it so well: "Surrender is not the best way to live; it is the only way to live. Nothing else works!"

True self-assurance will be yours when you yield your life to the Ultimate Source of confidence. This gift will not only be yours today, but for a lifetime. So, "[Be] confident of this very thing, that He who has begun a good work in you will complete it until the day of Jesus Christ" (Philippians 1:6).

This promise is for *you!*

 ## NOTES FOR YOUR SCORECARD

- Learn from experience until you master your subject.
- Remember, "You don't know what you don't know!"
- Be comfortable in your own skin.
- Never worry about things over which you have no control.
- Welcome competition, but the real battle is with yourself.
- Focus on your personal initiative, not the talent or abilities of someone else.
- Don't listen to your doubts; turn a deaf ear to negative voices.
- Surrender to the Ultimate Source of confidence.

TEE #8
EXPECTATIONS

*I*f you journey through life seeing the glass half empty, believing that tomorrow will be worse than today, that's the living environment you create for yourself. On the other hand, if you are filled with faith, hope, and confidence about the future, regardless of what happens, you'll wake up living in a better world. In the words of Sam Walton, founder of the retail giant Wal-Mart, "High expectations are the key to everything."

In this chapter we will focus on how to take charge of your hopes and dreams, the power of entering every arena of life with the anticipation of winning, and how positive belief defeats negative fear.

We will also examine the necessity of overcoming doubt, the art of adding action to your faith, how to adopt a vocabulary of expectation, and why you can look forward to receiving big blessings from a big God.

Let's tee off!

1. Take charge of your expectations

Over the years I have had the opportunity to interact with

one of the world's top sports psychologists, Bob Rotella. He has coached the winners of 74 major golf championships and works with many organizations, from the Cincinnati Reds in baseball to Joe Gibbs Racing in NASCAR.

It was enlightening and encouraging to hear him explain the power of the mind and why we should be careful what we allow to enter our sphere of thinking. Says Rotella, "You're either going to choose to believe in yourself or you're going to let doubt and uncertainty get in the way. Pretty soon, you're looking for a bad break instead of something good to happen. It just affects your whole outlook on life."

He emphasizes the necessity of controlling our thoughts and how we often permit the words of another to affect us, especially if what they say is harsh or negative.

Since what you feed grows, prepare a healthy meal for your mind.

2. Enter every arena with the expectation of winning

If you have ever watched the first few episodes of an *American Idol* season, you will see coliseums and arenas jammed with eager young people who have stars in their eyes and are brimming with hope. Some sing off-key and don't deserve to be at the audition, yet they believe with all their hearts they have what it takes to make the cut and live the dream.

As has been proven time and again, just because a contestant fails to win the top prize doesn't mean their efforts are wasted. Take the singer Mandisa, for example. On the fifth season of *American Idol* she finished in ninth place, yet today she is one of the best-selling Christian recording artists in the nation. I can't count the number of times I have listened to her songs, "Good Morning," and "Stronger" as part of my daily wake-up call. Her gift of music really speaks to me.

Golf tournaments, especially amateur events, are much like the *American Idol* process. Instead of walking away with a recording contract, golfers have a chance to compete and climb to the next level—hopefully the pinnacle, the PGA or LPGA tour. Only a few succeed, but without hope they wouldn't even try.

3. Positive expectation will defeat negative fear

Fear and anxiety are debilitating emotions. They are interest paid in advance on a debt we may never owe. Fear undermines faith—in ourselves, in others, and in God. It robs us of our potential, mires us in quicksand, and keeps us stagnate. Fear weakens, never strengthens, and is the breeder of even more fear.

During my study of Scripture, it became clear God is the

Father of psychology. For example we are told to "take captive every thought" to make it obedient to Christ (2 Corinthians 10:5), and we must think about what is true, noble, right, pure, and lovely (Philippians 4:8).

In order to lead a life of significance and be a difference-maker, we must be disciplined in winning what Joyce Meyers calls, "the battlefield of the mind."

God is not the author of anxiety, and negativity; He created each of us to fulfill our potential. In order to win, we must control what we "green light" ourselves to ponder. It is much easier to manage and maintain a positive attitude than it is to regain one. This is why we are told to "hold fast what is good" (1 Thessalonians 5:21).

4. The opposite of affirmative expectation is doubt

When you're standing alone on the tee box or out in the fairway, ready to hit a shot, doubt (the cousin of fear) can be a "death wish." As a golfing mom, I've learned that you have to be 100% sure—with total belief and commitment—in what you are about to do.

Sometimes when standing over a shot, a golfer can be "in-between clubs." This means he (or she) knows how far to hit the ball, but is unsure of which club to pull out of the bag to hit "that certain distance." For example, one club may be good for 170 yards and another for 200, but his distance reads 185.

He has to determine which club to pull and play the expectation game. He thinks, "Will I have to swing harder or lighter? What direction is the wind? Is it uphill or downhill? How hard or soft are the greens?"

After the golfer goes through this thought process, he must then step up and hit the shot. It is especially disconcerting if trouble lies ahead, such as a bunker, water hazard, a tree, tall grass, a drop off, etc. All these variables can cause a golfer to question his decision.

It has been said that negative expectation can only be removed by action—"pulling the trigger." This is how you learn, grow, and keep moving forward until you have faced the situation so many times that your problems turn to possibilities.

When you successfully defeat your mental enemy once, twice, then a hundred times, you develop the confidence and faith that the decision you are making is the right one. You believe in what you are about to do—and swooosh! The ball travels the right distance; no hooks, no slices, and lands exactly where you envisioned it would.

Another noted sports psychologist, Dr. Morris Pickens (called Dr. Mo), shared with me that to know how to handle doubt you have to put yourself in those settings enough times to overcome them. Familiarity creates a comfort zone for us.

Even if you make a mistake, remain optimistic and see the bright side. As Dr. Mo teaches, "After a missed or poor shot, say out loud an immediate positive reaction ('Give me a good lie!' 'Get a good bounce!' etc.). This helps you stay future focused, not past focused."

This also applies to life. As someone so brilliantly said, "Feed your faith, and doubt will starve to death."

5. Add action to your expectation

I can remember when God prompted me to begin writing my thoughts down on paper. So I bought a journal and started writing. Then the Lord said, "Why don't you share this with others?"

Next, I purchased a laptop and began sending out short paragraphs of inspiration on my personal Facebook page —praying they would be of help to those who happened to read them. I also wrote to the "inboxes" of friends and sent texts with words of encouragement to our children who were away at college and working.

The more I wrote, the better I felt, and the greater my belief and expectation grew. This step of faith and the feedback I received caused me to shed my doubts and keep going. It led to a website (wwwBack9Ministries.org), a daily blog, and much more.

It was like consuming an *Advocare Spark* energy drink when a reader would email and say, "Sherry, you have no idea what your post meant to me today." Or, "That was just what I needed."

Oh, there have been some negative comments—which can be expected when a blog is available to the public. I only pay attention to those with "constructive criticism." Then I do my best to learn from it, make a mental note, and forge ahead. This requires prayer because we can quickly find ourselves bogged down, focusing on the negative rather than the positive.

I have discovered that when I entertain positive outcomes and take action, my doubts shrink and my faith expands. I cling to what is written in Hebrews 11:16: "Without faith it is impossible to please Him, for he who comes to God must believe that He is, and that He is a rewarder of those who diligently seek Him." And I receive the counsel of James 1:6-8: "But let him ask in faith, with no doubting, for he who doubts is like a wave of the sea driven and tossed by the wind. For let not that man suppose that he will receive anything from the Lord; he is a double-minded man, unstable in all his ways."

Every day I pray for guidance from the Lord to give me the right words to say, and He continues to lead me.

Over my lifetime, faith, expectation, experience, and "pulling the trigger" are ingredients that have strengthened my "faith muscle"—which burns the "doubt fat." At the same time I trust God, bank on His promises, and see the results. This gives me the courage to continue walking forward, knowing that the Lord is with me every step of the way.

We have to move beyond wishing or hoping and take action regarding the purpose for which God has called us—school choice, academic major, career, marriage, parenting, etc.

Be careful not to receive the "gift of doubt" from those around you, or wallow in your own "self-doubt." This can cause deep scars. Please don't misunderstand me here. Pray, seek wise counsel, then make the decision God leads you toward. He stands ready and waiting; all you have to do is ask.

I love what the famous artist Vincent van Gogh said: "If you hear a voice within you say you cannot paint, then by all means paint and that voice will be silenced."

6. Adopt a vocabulary of expectation

There's an old adage, "Sticks and stones may break my bones, but words will never hurt me." I don't know who first came up with this quote, but they are absolutely wrong! If you break your arm, a doctor can put it in a cast and you'll be back to normal in a few weeks. But where is the surgeon who can mend a broken heart, or heal the emotional scars caused by someone who defames or lies about you?

Words not only wound, they can kill!

The Bible contains this powerful statement: "Death and life are in the power of the tongue" (Proverbs 18:21).

Once words spill out of our mouths, we own those statements forever. This is why Scripture warns: "Be quick to listen, slow to speak and slow to become angry, because human anger does not produce the righteousness that God desires" (James 1:19-20 NIV).

At times, dealing with the words of others has taken me to very dark places. It has caused me to reflect and examine my own vocabulary. It has stopped me dead in my tracks, made me ask myself, "Have I ever slain anyone with my sword of words?"

Anger is a very intense emotion that can be used to give us courage to stand up against wrongs, but it can often drive us to say and do things in the heat of the moment that we later deeply regret. Today, I am acutely aware and careful to "guard my heart"—because it is the source of everything I do and say.

Think of what happened in 2013 to Paula Dean, the popular celebrity chef. Because of using a racial term years earlier, she was fired from the *Food Network* and became the target of a massive negative attack by the media.

Of course she was wrong in her comment and the echo of her words will resonate for years—even though they are not a reflection of her today. Certainly people were hurt, but her honesty and remorse are evident. Our heavenly Father judges the motives of the heart, and those in the media should look at their own statements before casting the first stone. As we read in Proverbs 20:9-10, "Who can say, 'I have kept my heart pure; I am clean and without sin'? Differing weights and differing measures—the Lord detests them both."

It seems to me there is a modern day crucifixion of honesty taking place in our press. We all sin and fall short of the glory of the Lord (Romans 3:23), but we need to ask forgiveness, watch our words, and avoid repeating the same mistakes. That is the best anyone can do. Remember, Jesus said, "Let any one of you who is without sin be the first to throw a stone..." (John 9:7 NIV).

7. Expect big blessings from a Big God

Even though I had been a Christian and loved the Lord since the age of nine, a few years ago I realized that I had placed God in a box. In other words, the issues I was evidencing became so large that I relegated the Almighty to a place that was far smaller than He deserved.

Soon, I found myself on the sofa in a professional Christian counselor's office seeking solutions on how to depart from a destination I never intend to visit—but where I found myself.

I spent a lot of time in prayer, soul searching—allowing God to redefine my thinking. Through Scripture, like I had never known before, He infused me with new energy.

The first order of business for taking God out of the box was stepping back and looking at how in the world I had made the Lord so small that it had diminished my relationship with Him.

One day, the counselor gave me some advice that literally stunned me. He said, "Drop your hands." In other words, "Stop trying to solve all your problems yourself. Give the Lord a chance."

As I became completely honest with myself, God, and the Christian counselor, I started seeing how I was trying to play God, being in charge of others, rather than allowing the Lord to work.

I was reminded that, according to Scripture, when I stand before the Lord and give an account of my life, no one will be standing with me; I will be there alone. As 2 Corinthians 5:10 tells us: "For we must all appear before the judgment seat of Christ, that each one may receive the things done in the body, according to what he has done, whether good or bad."

This painted a clear and vivid picture of a new path I was to follow—a path more concerned with my relationship with the Lord and obedience. My focus shifted away from trying to be responsible for other people and their actions.

The second order of business for me was to get up earlier, *much* earlier, and spend more time, *much* more time, with the Lord. As I detailed earlier in this book, this time included reading the Bible, praying, and sitting quietly before a holy

God. The Lord was leading me to this and I knew it was the right thing to do. But somehow over time and the demands of life, I made God ride shotgun instead of letting Him be the driver.

I'm far from where I want to be (and know I won't be complete until I reach heaven), but the fruit of being honest with myself and God has deepened my intimate relationship with Him.

> *Learning to praise God in the hard times ensures you won't forget Him in the good times.*

Day after day, I tell the Lord, "I will hope continually, and will praise You yet more and more" (Psalm 71:14).

This has taken me from the path of being a "people pleaser," to the road of being a "God pleaser"—including the launching of a ministry.

When I took God out of the box, He gave me the solid foundation He intends for all of us to stand on. He is the source of our hope.

Today, start living the words of the psalmist: "My soul, wait silently for God alone, for my expectation is from Him" (Psalm 62:5).

Why sabotage your future? There is no substitute for faith, belief, hope, and positive anticipation.

NOTES FOR YOUR SCORECARD

- Take charge of your expectations by looking for something good to happen.
- Enter every arena with the anticipation of winning.
- Conquer fear by defeating your doubts over and over again.
- Add action to your expectation.
- Watch your words. Adopt a hope-filled vocabulary.
- Drop your hands. Stop trying to do everything yourself.
- Expect big blessings from a big God.

TEE #9
TOMORROW

*A*s we reach the "turn," completing the Front Nine of our course in life, it's time to be thankful for how far we have come, and to get excited about the future.

On this tee we will see the importance of preparing for tomorrow by taking care of today. We will also discuss how God's angels are ready and able to help us, the steps to discovering the divine plan for our lives, the key to a fear-free horizon, plus the necessity of being prepared for our meeting with the Lord.

BLOOM WHERE YOU ARE PLANTED!

When I was young, I didn't live in a neighborhood. Our farm had large pastures in front and back, so when I walked out any door, the first thing I usually saw were cows, not people! But my adult life has been much different—moving from a small town to the capital city of our state with a home on a cul-de-sac.

I love it, but there are days when I miss the rural life and

145

the benefits of wide open spaces. During the past quarter-century we've lived in two great neighborhoods and the friends we have made are wonderful blessings.

Of course, there are many different personalities, backgrounds, lifestyles, and interests, but the variety has enriched my journey and world tremendously.

Just a few days ago, a neighbor sent out an email, inviting anyone who might be home to stop by for a social get-together. It was a blast—catching up with people we usually just greet in passing.

Some time back, while entertaining a small gathering at our home on a Friday night, I received an alarming call from another neighbor. She was riding in an ambulance with her oldest son, who had been severely injured in his high school football game. Her voice was shaking as she asked for prayer.

The young man was close to our family, and had described me as his "Second Mama"—which I accepted as an extreme compliment.

He became the center of our concern and I am happy to report that our prayers were answered. After several surgeries, his leg and foot have healed.

I have come to embrace what the Apostle Paul wrote in Galatians 5:14: "For all the law is fulfilled in one word, even in this: 'You shall love your neighbor as yourself.'"

I realize this passage is referring to more than individuals who reside on our street, but we can't all travel to the ends of the earth, so we are called to "bloom where we are planted!"

What a privilege to walk the extra mile for our neighbors. Our willingness to be a friend can be of untold significance.

We must show our care and concern today, and be ready to respond to the needs of others tomorrow.

I BELIEVE IN ANGELS!

Recently I was asked, "Sherry, do you believe in angels?" Without a moment's hesitation, I emphatically answered, "Yes!"

I am firmly convinced that these heavenly beings have been sent by God in the past, are present with us right now, and are waiting to help us in the future.

Angels are referenced more than 270 times in the Bible and, according to Scripture, are under God's control and subject to Christ. They serve the purpose of messengers, military (war and protection), and ministry, but they are not meant to be worshiped.

- God's angel appeared as a messenger to Joseph when he learned that his "promised wife" was pregnant (Matthew 1:20).
- God's angel spoke to Gideon to encourage him (Judges 6:12).
- When Daniel was thrown into the lion's den, God sent His angel to shut the mouths of the lions (Daniel 6:22).
- The angel, Michael, battled the king of Persia to deliver a message to Daniel (Daniel 10:13).
- Peter was sleeping, confined in prison when the Lord sent an angel to wake him up. His chains fell off and he was free (Acts 12:7)—and there are many more examples.

We may not realize it, because we do not physically see them, but there are angels in our midst. They are all around us. As stated in Hebrews 13:2, "Do not forget to entertain strangers, for by so doing some have unwittingly entertained angels."

The noted evangelist, Billy Graham, made this statement: "We must be aware that angels keep in close and vital contact with all that is happening on the earth. Their knowledge of earthly matters exceeds that of me. Let us believe that they are here among us."

It is marvelous to read what is written in God's Word and acknowledged by others, but I became convinced that angels are real because of what happened in our own home.

I mentioned earlier how our son, Thomas, was diagnosed with Type 1 diabetes when he was just five years old.

After he was released from the hospital, I lacked experience in knowing how to take care of him—and Thomas was too young to communicate his physical feelings or have a true understanding of what was happening. We had enough new knowledge to know that "night time and sleep" were dangerous hours because he could be resting and have a diabetic "low" or "high." Either one can be harmful and deadly.

My husband and I set the alarm to wake up each night to check his blood sugar about every two hours. We were in a constant state of exhaustion.

One night, two weeks after Thomas came home, shortly after drifting off to sleep, I abruptly woke up thinking that Bill had called out my name. I heard, "Sherry," and sat up like a bolt out of the blue, asking "What? What?"

But Bill was out like a light, sound asleep next to me. I looked around to see if anyone else was standing by the bed, and then I got up. It was an eerie feeling. I just knew I had heard my name being called.

I immediately decided, since I was wide awake, I would check on the boys. It wasn't time to monitor Thomas, but I went to have a look anyway. His glucometer read "LOW!"

Please understand; since Thomas was diagnosed we'd had low numbers of 20s and 30s. but it had never registered

"LOW" before—let alone flashing. I quickly grabbed the emergency gel and frantically started squeezing it into his mouth. I massaged his lifeless cheeks as tears started to flow down my face. I then rechecked, and it read "20," still dangerously low. There was no time to arouse Bill, so I kept administering gel and massaging. A few minutes later it was up to "30." After two hours of this, his blood sugar slowly, very slowly, rose to a normal level of "120."

I sat by his bedside for the rest of the night, and I have to admit it took a long time for me to regain a semblance of calm . But in the dark, morning hours, I began to find comfort in the fact that I had heard my name.

With all my heart, I believe the Lord sent an angel to awaken me for the protection of our son.

This knowledge of God's safe-keeping sustained me as Thomas reached the age where he could drive on his own, get on an airplane by himself (with no one knowing he was diabetic), and going off to college.

I have often reflected on the fact that I distinctly heard my name, "Sherry!" My kids would have said, "Mom," and it wasn't my husband, because he was fast asleep. Without question, the voice that called my name was an angel!

I don't know when or where
you will need the warning or protection
of ministering angels, but God does
—and He will send them to you.

GOD HAS A PLAN

As a mother watching all three of our children chase and pursue their dreams—and sometimes becoming discouraged in the process—I have found myself telling them, "God has a plan."

He placed each one of us here for a unique mission. Let me remind you that "we are God's handiwork, created in Christ Jesus to do good works, which God prepared in advance for us to do" (Ephesians 2:10 NIV).

Rebelling against the Lord's sovereign plan has consequences. Think of Jonah, who God specifically told to journey to the city of Nineveh, but being afraid, he headed in the opposite direction. Because of his disobedience, Jonah ended up in the belly of a whale and had a few unpleasant days to think about his life and choices. He was ultimately given a second chance to follow God's blueprint instead of his own.

The underlying problem was that Jonah allowed his fear to guide his original actions. And remember, most fear is not from God. "Do not be afraid; do not be discouraged. Be strong and courageous. This is what the Lord will do to all the enemies you are going to fight" (Joshua 10:25 NIV).

In golf, I have seen our children become unnerved before hitting a shot; one they may have practiced a thousand times. Satan will weave his web of words and trick them into believing the following lies:

- "Will I get cursed out for hitting this shot?" Fear of man!
- "What will people think if I don't execute this well?" Fear of other's opinions!
- "What if I don't hit it where I want to?" Fear of failure!
- "What if I don't sink this putt that everyone expects me to make?" Fear, fear, fear!

The message I have done my best to instill in our family is that we are not to fear man but we must have respect and a reverent fear of Almighty God. As the psalmist wrote thousands of years ago, "The Lord is on my side; I will not fear. What can man do to me?" (Psalm 118:6).

Of course, there is healthy fear that prevents us from doing foolish things such as diving in shallow water"—where the result could be a broken neck.

However, the enemy is hell-bent on inflicting upon us unhealthy fear to the extent that we develop a lack of trust that God will take us to the other side.

Even the chosen disciples faced this problem. They knew Jesus well and had seen Him perform amazing miracles, but when a storm arose on the Sea of Galilee, they were terrified—even though the Lord was with them in the boat. The end result was that Jesus spoke a word and calmed the tempest (Matthew 8:23-27).

While on earth, Jesus was fully man and fully God. He exhibited the emotions of compassion, sadness, and anger, but there is no account of fear in His life. Why? Because He operated through His Father, God.

What an example! Make it your objective to keep your eyes on Jesus, the "Author and Perfecter" of your faith (Hebrews 12:2). Examine your fears and seek daily to hand them over to the Lord.

Take heart in this truth: "God has not given us a spirit of fear, but of power and of love and of a sound mind" (2 Timothy 1:7). We also know, "There is no fear in love, but perfect love casts out fear."

*Only one path leads to a fear-free future.
Don't worry about tomorrow; put your faith
and trust in the Prince of Peace.*

LIVE LIKE YOU ARE DYING

When we lay our heads on our pillows at night, none of us know what tomorrow will bring.

I have often thought about the phrase and song, "Live like you are dying." I don't mean to sound morbid, but if we all would wake up every morning and face that reality, perhaps we would approach life a little differently. We might start thinking about eternity, and hopefully value each day more.

As I watched my parents age and have attended the funerals of dear friends who have passed away, it has caused me to evaluate how I live.

Let me share the story of a friend who got life right.

As a freshman at Clemson I pledged the Tri Delta sorority. One of the requirements on the check-list was to get to know all the sisters (upper-classmen) in the sorority by interviewing them and obtaining their signatures. I remember meeting Kathleen Crouch, a senior, one Friday morning. She was in her room, packing for a trip to visit her boyfriend, Jon, who played football for the University of North Carolina.

Kathleen was beautiful, sweet-natured and I loved getting to know her. She gave me tips about college and sorority life. In fact, that entire year she was an encouragement to me and a role model. Little did I know that we would both marry men who grew up as best friends.

In July 2013, I attended the funeral of Kathleen's husband, Jon—one of Bill's buddies. They had shared much together and Jon was even in our wedding. The atmosphere at the funeral was inspiring. Jon was the oldest son of Jerry Richardson, owner of the Carolina Panthers NFL football team.

Hundreds of people were packed into the Forest Hill Church in Charlotte, North Carolina, for the memorable service—including many notables.

Jon's brother, Mark, and a dear friend, Joan, who attended Clemson University while I was there, introduced

Bill and me on a blind date my junior year. Needless to say, there's a long-time friendship with this family. There is always sadness when a life passes, but I knew his funeral would be a joyful celebration of a man who lived life *large* in God's eyes, and in mine.

At the service, three men stood to honor Jon and testify of his outstanding contributions. The first was Mike Bunkley, an African-American who was a former Panthers team chaplain. Through his tears, Mike told of Jon's generosity. Mike shared that while he was on the staff of the Panthers, he would often find anonymous notes of encouragement on his desk. For years, those motivating words kept him going. He discovered much later that it was Jon who had written them.

The next tribute was from a Richardson family friend, Davis Kuykendall. He spoke of how Jon had the ability to be "all there" when he was with someone—making that person feel like family. Davis went so far as to ask those present to stand if they felt like they were one of Jon's best friends. Over 90 percent of the large audience stood and erupted into lengthy applause.

He also shared how Jon provided one-on-one mentoring and tutoring to underprivileged children in the Charlotte area. I was crying and smiling at the same time as he spoke of the value Jon put on people and relationships.

He lived out the phrase, "Your actions are so loud, I can't hear what you are saying!"

The final eulogy came from Jon's pastor, David Chadwick. He commented, "There are many things I could say, but I want to honor Jon's request to share the Gospel today." He proceeded to do this eloquently and unapologetically.

You see, Jon became a Christian as an adult, after he was diagnosed with cancer. (He battled this disease for nearly 13 years.)

Chadwick concluded Jon's life celebration by quoting the renowned British preacher John Wesley: "Give me one hundred men who fear nothing but sin, and desire nothing but God, and I care not a straw whether they be clergymen or laymen; such alone will shake the gates of hell and set up the kingdom of heaven on Earth."

Jon, with humility, generosity, and a love for who Christ was and what He had done for him, was a world changer! He lived 1 John 2:15-17: "Do not love the world or anything in the world. If anyone loves the world, the love of the Father is not in them. For everything in the world—the lust of the flesh, the lust of the eyes, and the pride of life—comes not from the Father but from the world. The world and its desires pass away, but whoever does the will of God lives forever" (NIV).

His was a life worth living.

The impact of that day will always stay with me, The words of a song I heard years ago are ones we should all live by: "Many things about the future, I don't seem to understand. But I know Who holds tomorrow, and I know Who holds my hand."

NOTES FOR YOUR SCORECARD

- By showing love to your neighbors today, you'll be ready to help them tomorrow.
- Bloom where you are planted!
- God's angels are with us now, and are ready to protect and minister to us in the future.
- The Lord has a plan for your path ahead.
- Only God can give you a future that is fear free.
- Live with eternity in view.

MAKE EACH SHOT COUNT!

The *Front Nine* in life has brought hundreds of lessons to my doorstep: some from victories, some from defeats, and others from just living. There is an old adage, "It is not how you start but how you finish."

Heading into the *Back Nine* of life, I reflect and understand this to mean, "enjoy a life of significance, but don't forget to enjoy the process along the way." Bask in the "spotlight moments," yet realize they are fleeting—and always remember Who allowed you to be there.

A country song, "You're Gonna Miss This," by Trace Adkins, describes the reflective thoughts of a parent whose child is wishing their life away. The lyrics include:

These are some good times,
So take a good look around.
You may not know it now,
But you're gonna miss this.

Don't wish your life away pining for the future. Enjoy the process and make each shot count! It is God who orders your steps and places opportunities in your path, but it is your choice to embrace them.

Remember, "today is the tomorrow of yesterday." I pray you will live each day to its fullest potential. There is a bright future ahead!

To Schedule the Author
for Speaking Engagements, Contact:
www.Back9Ministries.org